PLEASE WIPE

B

Stanley George

Copyright © Stanley George 2015

The right of Stanley George to be identified as the author of this work has been asserted to him in accordance with the Copyright, Designs and Patents act 1988. All rights reserved.

This publication or any part of it may not be reproduced or stored in any way without prior written permission of the author.

The irreverent, humorous, misadventures of a GPO apprentice and paraffin entrepreneur

This is a tale of the humorous misadventures of a new apprentice. From selling dodgy paraffin as a young weekend hopeful, to the early years of non-work with the GPO.

A mixture of fact and fiction that will leave you guessing; did they really do that?

Now, be warned, some sections contain events of a sexual nature! You will also notice expletives used often throughout most dialogues. This is because, to be frank, these words were used in abundance. It was not even considered swearing. In fact many of the guys would use them as adjectives in every sentence. I felt that inclusion gave a better flavour of the period.

Just to set the scene here are a few things that were happening around these times,

Alf Ramsey was knighted for winning the World Cup for England, We won the Eurovision song contest, The UK applied for EEC membership, Charles de Gaulle vetoed our membership!, The Beatles released Sergeant Pepper, Concorde was

unveiled in Toulouse, Demonstrations were held in London against Vietnam and the M1 motorway was finally completed.

Finally just a few legal notes,

Any mention of money taken without payment of tax is, of course, pure fiction. In fact all normally paid Saturday work, undertaken by myself and others, was undertaken for free. This was clearly just a favour for a friend.

Any item mentioned as stolen is pure fiction. Nobody in London would dream of illegally taking anything from an employer or anyone else for that matter. Everyone mentioned in this book was completely honest at all times.

All seemingly illegal actions undertaken in the telephone exchange; including actions contra to the official secrets act, are pure fiction. Nobody working for the GPO would ever undertake anything illegal such as listening to people's calls, winding back meters, growing cannabis or fiddling with special branch recording devices.

All mention of laziness or GPO individuals being work shy is pure fiction. These gentlemen were hard working, conscientious, and knowledgeable. Their every waking breath was aimed at providing customer satisfaction.

All the names of true individuals have been changed to protect those innocent folk from confusion or legal proceedings. For those that are actually now dead and beyond retribution; yes they did it.

The sequence of some late 60's events have been slightly adjusted. This was to condense the misadventures into a meaningful flow.

Sometimes truth can be stranger than fiction thus I have used fiction to water down the truth.

Table of Contents

CHAPTER 1- Beginnings, Wigs and Esso Blue

CHAPTER 2-Tests, Slate and Parking Pain

CHAPTER 3-Pink Cake and Pay Deductions

CHAPTER 4-The Exchange, Grades and Hats

CHAPTER 5-Work Clothes, Tools and The Boss

CHAPTER 6-Jumpers, Siesta and Slack-Back

CHAPTER 7-Derek's Eggs and Paddy's Brains

CHAPTER 8-Limping Store Men and Face Masks

CHAPTER 9-Double Chins and Line Ups

CHAPTER 10-Requisition Mayhem and Swarfega

CHAPTER 11-Dirty Jobs and a Wage Snatch

CHAPTER 12-Butt Resistance and Listening In

CHAPTER 13-Idle Pastimes and Sex Shows

CHAPTER 14-Bad Timing and Washer Japes

CHAPTER 15-Suntans, Meters and FNF

CHAPTER 16-Cable Chamber Secrets and Porn

CHAPTER 17-Batteries, Drugs and Funerals

CHAPTER 18-Fuses, Megger and Pistol Fun

CHAPTER 19-External Holes and Climbing Poles

CHAPTER 20-Kiosk Scams and Drawing Pins

CHAPTER 21-Oildag and Flooding Woes

CHAPTER 22-Fire Proof Sacks and Physical Jerks

CHAPTER 23-Sick Leave and All's Quiet

CHAPTER 24-Kite Chaos and Winning Horses

CHAPTER 25-Spotty Mystery & First Aid Scam

EPILOGUE

CHAPTER 1- Beginnings, Wigs and Esso Blue

Now here's a thing, what led you to your first job? Was it money, power, ambition or was it just a general interest?

Well, I can not recall the actual moment when the GPO developed as a great career idea, but I guess a visit from an old friend started it. He mentioned his very attractive £6.50 weekly wage as a new GPO engineering apprentice. Plus he expanded on the GPO's laid back, work shy ethic. That just about sold it. I was, and still am, work averse. Not necessarily being work shy; rather, not wishing to contemplate it too much!

Having just emerged from a rather large, lack lustre comprehensive school; I had given no thought to the looming prospect of actually working full time for a living. I had grimly hung on to the safety of the school ethos where nothing was expected and less given.

In fact, the only positive thing ever to come from Brooke House School was Alan Sugar. That just about sums the place up. I still haven't forgiven him for the dodgy Amstrad computer his company sold me. I should have known better.

However, getting back to the prospect of an apprenticeship with the GPO; let's put this potential £6.50 in perspective. In the late 60s beer was 10p a pint, cigarettes were 20p a pack and you could get 4 gallons of petrol for a £1. So, £6.50 would do, as long as I continued to exploit my free board and lodging at home.

Petrol, of course, was not a great worry to a teenager then. My mode of transport was a motorbike not a car. Great on mileage, low on insurance and bloody dangerous. My latest motorbike was an AJS 250 which, much to the dread of my parents, was my pride and joy. Also, I had the fall-back of a second job during the winter. This was selling poor quality paraffin to an unsuspecting Stoke Newington public at the weekend.

This job as a paraffin entrepreneur may not equate to your idea of work averse. But believe me the work was short term, hilarious, the rewards high, and the responsibilities zero. However, you could smell my work clothes from 100 metres.

In those days paraffin was a popular heating method. It was smelly but cheap and as I was to discover later; hazardous. Lets face it paraffin was widely used as jet fuel and powered some rocket engines. So, on reflection, using it to heat your home was slightly precarious to say the least. It also was notoriously smelly. As we came and went delivering the paraffin, each opened door presented a waft of burning oil.

At the time there were two major companies for paraffin, both competing for the same customers. Aladdin Pink came from Shell and Esso produced their version, Esso Blue. A smaller third offering called Regent Green never really made it.

As you might guess from the description both Aladdin pink and Esso Blue were identified by their trade colour. They bombarded the unsuspecting public with many adverts displaying the unique qualities of their product. Less smell, cleaner burn and longer lasting.

Esso Blue made it to the top of the tree with its television adverts with their catchy jingle and cartoon character called Joe. Inevitably, on the round, most of the customers called me Joe and thought it hilarious.

Both colours had their following and, as is usual, some folk would never swap one for the other. As you will see, the reality for us was very different.

We picked up the delivery tanker from the fuel depot, filling her up from the vast storage tanks rusting in the yard. This depot was tucked away in a backstreet in Hackney. It supplied paraffin to a motley selection of characters. Most of who looked as though they had stepped out of a Dickens book. The place had an air of mystery topped off by a surround of barbed wire coated walls.

The ground always looked like liquid mud. This was not due to water; this was the by-product of years of paraffin spillage. Not a place to spend too much time in safety, thus we were mostly in and out fast.

The ageing tanker had one big tank split into two compartments, both holding more than 500 gallons. Into these we pumped the paraffin, clear as water, from a supplier as mysterious as the Mary Celeste. Then dye was thrown into each compartment, blue into one and pink in the other. Our bumpy ride to the first customer provided the scientific method of mixing.

The tanker had many adverts stuck to its sides declaring the benefits of Shell and Esso. But the actual origin of the paraffin will never be known.

We often would run out of Blue and have to persuade the customer to buy Pink. This was usually followed, the next week, by disgruntled complaints about how the Pink was not as good. It was smelly and apparently didn't last as long! Little did they know it was all the same!

How I actually was introduced to this enterprise came purely by location. The block of flats where we lived, Gibson Gardens, had its share of entrepreneurs. Two of these sold paraffin to regular customers throughout Stoke Newington and Hackney. This was achieved by driving 'seen better days' fuel tankers through the streets and selling their contents.

I started by helping the smaller of these enterprises before being poached by the major operator, George. My first paraffin boss, Besty, was a lorry driver by trade. He spent most of his time 'removing' goods from his lorry for onward resale. He was, therefore, always losing one job only to be picked up on another. He later appeared in the local press for using his children to ferry handguns around various London gangs. He shortly afterwards mysteriously disappeared from the 'Gardens' and I never saw him again.

Gibson Gardens itself is worth a further mention as this was my base for all the coming adventures. Picture, if you will, a drab Victorian red brick block of flats tucked away from the main road in Stoke Newington. All this protected by large imposing black iron gates at the front, and a railway at the back. A helpful large sign was cemented into the brickwork by the main gates stating;

"Built in 1880 by the Metropolitan Association for improving the dwellings of the industrial classes."

Thinking about the words on that sign now, I am not sure if the iron gates were to keep intruders out or to keep the 'industrial classes' in! And as for improving the dwellings; these flats did not even have a bathroom just a tiny loo located in the kitchen!

Bathing was something you did, in front of the fire in a tin bath. Not too great for me for, as the youngest, I was fourth in the queue. The only alternative was a weekly treat of a venture down to

Clissold Road Public Baths. Here you could partake in the luxury of a real bath. Albeit timed, rather run down and a bit smelly.

At the side of the flats, next to the black gates, was a small corner shop. This was the domain of Mr & Mrs Prentice. The corner shop sold everything from sliced ham to Players Weights cigarettes, and was a massive help in times of need. A tab could be stretched several weeks before payment. A demand for one or two cigarettes only was never refused. The only downside was the language! Mrs Prentice used the expletive 'fuck' almost every other word. It was indiscriminate and took no notice of age or gender. As a very young lad I learned more swear words in that shop than most dockers use in a lifetime!

What on earth was the Metropolitan Association thinking when the design of Gibson Gardens was put forward? Here we had hundreds of very small, two bedroom flats with no bathrooms. They had paper thin walls and were constructed right next to the railway line. I would love to have been at their planning meeting.

Comfortably snuggled in a leather chair, cigar in one hand and brandy in the other, they discussed the plan,

"Do working class chappies actually wash?" enquires an honourable member.

"Damn it man, of course not," replies the chairman.

"Don't want to make these chappies feel bad about being working class you know," adds the member.

"That is not a problem old chap, we going to call them *industrial* classes," explains the chairman!

Of course, time moves on and these flats have now been completely renovated. Externally the original buildings remain. The iron gates still stand proud. Even the quaintly cobbled street is still there. But now the flats have either had two flats knocked into one; with bathroom. Or they have been made into a one bedroom modern abode. They are now in the hands of yuppies or first time buyers and are sold for £350,000 a time. (These are 2015 prices and rising!)

The 'industrial classes' sign has long since gone and with it an era of innocence, fun and a feeling of looking after one another.

Every London block of flats, like Gibson Gardens,

had its Del boy character and George the paraffin boss was ours. He was always on the look out for the next scam and always on the make. He seemed to know every crook in London. A feat I disbelieved at first. However as time went on, and various notorious local characters stopped us in the street for a chat, it was clear that he probably did.

He was about 50 at the time but was as fit as a 30 year old. This was testament, I think, to hard graft out in the fresh air. In fact, his favourite saying was, "Only indoor flowers wilt!"

His Achilles heal was his hair, or lack of it. And he persisted in wearing a cheap 'syrup', or wig to non-Londoners, which simply looked daft. He did however negate this appearance by always wearing a flat cap over it. Sometimes, when lifting his hat to a passing lady, his wig would come off too. This caused much hilarity for me, the lady in question and to be fair to him as well.

I can picture him now standing there laughing with a cigarette dangling out of one corner of his mouth. He always wore a thick brown leather bomber jacket over white mechanics overalls; large boots, flat cap and a cravat tied round the throat. His every movement caused a waft of paraffin essence to attack the senses.

He drove an expensive car and was definitely the local Lothario. As to why he lived in Gibson Gardens is beyond me. Perhaps he felt at home amongst the other working class folk. It certainly provided plenty of local 'crumpet' to chase. An entertainment he seemed to continually partake in. Unfortunately, the local 'crumpet' in question was always married and we had no end of ducking and diving to do whilst on the paraffin round.

His love of expensive cars was mirrored by his hate of small ones. Mini cars were his 'bête noire' and every time he saw one he would call out,

"You need one of those on each foot, plonker!"

Another hate was dog crap. He maintained that dogs would be alright if they didn't have arseholes. He continually pointed out the offending piles as we wandered the streets and seemed to have an unexplained knowledge of their pedigree. He would shock passers by rigid with,

"Got a slice of bread matey?" while pointing at a large steaming addition to the Stoke Newington pavement. This, of course, was only done when someone was in suitable earshot.

Another favourite trick was to dangle a lit cigarette from his mouth while pouring paraffin into a serving can. Then, in front of the horrified customer, drop it in. Most dived for cover as he laughed at the joke. Of course paraffin didn't ignite like petrol so all was cool; but I am sure we had a few soiled pants along our route.

I joined George's motley crew as a young teenager. Too young to be doing this sort of work, but money is money at any age. Plus this really didn't seem like work. My job, along with other lads that came and went, was to collect the paraffin cans from homes along the route. Then get them filled at the tanker returning them to the customer for payment.

Carrying a 5 gallon can up several flights of stairs did wonders for my growing biceps and left the skin on my hands like leather. The remnants of this hard skin still remain today.

To both forewarn our pending customers, and relay our presence to potential new ones, we shouted "OIL" as we wandered up and down. This came out more like "Oi-YELL!" as we projected the call the length of the street. This projection technique resurfaced much later when a brief, fruitful acting career materialised. I found that I could appear to speak quietly on stage, while being clearly heard at the back of the theatre.

We met and served many amazing London characters on the paraffin round. And, I received an education in dealing with people that served me well through life. These characters could range from brothel madams to houses with 10 families, and from middle class wealth to stinking hovels. We served them all and saw it all. And you're going to meet some of them along the way.

CHAPTER 2-Tests, Slate and Parking Pain

So, back with my prospect of £6.50 from the GPO, I had now decided to bite the bullet. After a quick check in a friend's phone book, I uncovered the appropriate address for applications. A demand for an application form was quickly responded to. It arrived in days. Now with the application duly filled out and posted I nonchalantly waited for their rush to my door.

A letter arrived some time later inviting me to arrive at Crouch End Telephone House for an interview. Thus my fate was sealed. The strange thing is I never doubted getting this job. It was the only interview I attended and no other career was contemplated. These were days when getting a job was easy. It was actually avoiding one that was hard!

I had, while at school, attended a couple of visits to gain working life experience. The career adviser could not have picked two worse examples of the terror that is work. The first was a heavy engineering plant. The heat was unbearable, the people greasy and covered in sweat. Plus the work was obviously tough. The whole group of school kids all came out shell shocked, as did the career adviser as well.

The second visit was an ill fated trip to HMS Ganges in Suffolk. This royal navy training establishment opened my eyes to the torture inflicted on its unfortunate inhabitants. They were shouted at, pushed, shoved and generally verbally abused; and this was just to get them into the canteen! Plus, all the time I was there, a 143 feet high mast loomed over everything. A mast these young cadets were going to climb!

I had already made my mind up about this place as we made our way to the canteen for a parting cup of tea. The young guys inside all whispered the same message,

"Don't join, it's a fucking nightmare!"

A message I did not need to be told twice.

So, it was to be the GPO. I arrived at Crouch End Telephone House on the appointed day. Parked the motorbike in someone's parking space and was ushered into a large room. Sitting quietly inside were 15 or so other lads, all looking a bit concerned. Tables and chairs were arranged and we were asked to take our places for a test. Now, this followed closely on from taking a variety of CSE/GCE examinations at school. So, it did not faze me too much. Albeit that I had screwed up most of my exams through a combination of laziness and pure indifference.

The actual test was a mixture of simple maths, spelling and some general knowledge. All of which I completed quite quickly. Looking up I expected satisfied nods from all of the participants. I was very wrong. Puzzled faces, displaying mild panic combined with distant stares, greeted me. These guys, for the most part, were really struggling. To make matters worse, in true GPO style, these test papers were marked in our presence.

A deathly silence hung over the room like a fog while a young female clerk totted up the results. Four of us were politely requested to remain. The others were politely requested not to! This was my first wake up call. In the real world not everyone gets a job! And, if you cannot even get a job with the GPO where do you try next?

The remaining applicants were then ushered into a waiting room and informed to expect an interview. We, of course, shared our experiences of the test paper and agreed that only a complete dick head could have failed it. It did not occur to me at the time that, as was highly probable, only complete dick heads were actually applying.

We were called in one at a time for an interview with the Executive Engineer. This sounded pretty grand to me. The title alone was impressive. I learned later that the GPO, aka the Civil Service, simply loved all things to do with grades, levels and job titles.

The clerk, showing me into the interview room, whispered something about 'listening carefully' as I went through the door. This was, in fact, not a wise tip on interview techniques, it was a warning. The Executive Engineer was a complete buffoon who could hardly be understood. Each sentence started well enough, but quickly became quieter and quieter. It was like he was falling slowly asleep as the sentence went on.

I, of course, leaned closer and closer during each sentence. By the end of two minutes I was close enough to smell his breath, and all became clear. I think the nautical expression *'three sheets to the wind'* sums it up. For those not from a nautical background; he was pissed!

At one stage he threw a piece of splayed telephone cable onto the table,

"Tell me what those colours are," he demanded.

Now this seemed easy enough. Red, white, blue, green, grey......

"What did you say then?" he interrupted.

"Grey," I innocently responded.

"It's SLATE, not bloody grey," he shouted.

This guy was clearly here under sufferance. He needed to get back to the pub and we were in his way. He closed the rather brief interview by simply telling me that I would do. And I was led away.

The clerk must have heard the shout. She kindly explained that everyone gets asked that question and everyone gets it wrong. This was my first introduction, in fact, to GPO speak! This question with the cable was, believe or not, their scientific method of testing for colour blindness!

Just to finish off the perfect day, someone had stuck a piece of paper on my motorbike. This politely informed me to, *'leave your fucking bike in somebody else's place, knob head!'* Welcome to the GPO.

By the time I got home again I was somewhat confused as to whether I had actually got the job or not. This meant waiting several nervous days for the post to deliver the result. It finally arrived and I had been offered the apprenticeship plus given a date to start.

By start, of course, they meant back to Crouch End Telephone House for an induction briefing. Now, I did not relish going back there again too quickly and was beginning to get second thoughts. However winter was not yet here and the paraffin round was a couple of months away. So off I went again to Crouch End; money had called.

CHAPTER 3-Pink Cake and Pay Deductions

This time I was more selective in the parking arrangements. By this I mean I parked the motorbike two streets away. On entry I was again ushered into the same room as before; once more to join a group of others. We were, apparently, this year's intake for the GPO North Area Telephones.

A more disparate group you will never meet. Little did I know then that, by the end of our first year, one would nearly cut off both his feet, another would lose a finger and worse still one would die in an accident. That does not even include my own near-death experience with my motorbike.

It was not till many years later that this 'numbers game' became clear. An unfortunate necessity, in a future role, was to write condolence letters to the families of engineers killed on the job. When you have an organisation with a couple of hundred thousand employees; not all of them make it to the end of the year!

The first day proceedings started well enough, a welcoming chat from a senior manager, and a cup of tea. They even threw in some pink cake as well.

I spent decades confronting this pink cake at various meetings and events. I never fathomed out what it was supposed to taste of, what it was made with or where it came from. It was always there. It must have been a Civil Service thing.

Next we had a talk by the union representative. At this stage the guy who had greeted us, left. It was clear that there was some friction between the two of them. I still remember the union guy's name as I bumped into him from time to time; Brian. In a much later role, when we had both risen in parallel hierarchies, I pretty much destroyed him during a negotiation on overtime.

I was at this meeting representing British Telecom Human Resources and Brian, knowing my background, unbelievably allowed a younger union colleague to lean aggressively forward and shout,

"The trouble with you is you don't know what it's like out there!"

"Actually I do my friend, get your background checks right. In fact I invented half the overtime scams your guys are pulling at the moment!" I helpfully responded.

Brian whispered something urgent in his colleague's ear; they changed tack and lost the plot. He retired soon after and never spoke to me again!

Back at the Crouch End induction, with his audience of naive apprentices, Brian immediately went on the attack. How we needed his help to survive. How we would need to join the union to stave off sackings and bad treatment from the management. How we would never get a pay rise without the union etc. etc. This, of course, was a bit of a shock given our lack of industry experience. It also explained why our senior manager host had left!

Was our life really going to be this tough? Very quickly we all signed the proffered union document. This gave our permission to have the union subscription taken directly from our weekly pay. His job done, Brian was gone.

Next we enjoyed the first of many smoke breaks experienced in my life at work. I had never come across this before. A break to smoke a cigarette seems almost criminal now. Then there followed the highlight of the day; working clothes measurement.

The clothes in question comprised firstly, one large black woollen overcoat. This had GPO in red on each collar and large black buttons helpfully also marked GPO. Next came the red safety helmet also carefully marked GPO on the front. Third came the boots with GPO in red on each side and finally a large brown leather 'Gladstone' tool bag with, yes you're ahead of me, GPO printed boldly on the side.

I think that they were trying to tell us something; we were now the property of the GPO. However, in true Civil Service style, all this was to be made redundant. In October 1969 the GPO ceased to be a government department. It was established as a public corporation under the heading Post Office Telecommunications. The term GPO was gone, all things green were to become yellow and ...er!...nothing else changed.

Now, none of these items were for us to take on the day. These were 'display' items. Ours would arrive later. So, to move this on we each underwent careful measurement from the stores representative.

I would have been a bit more hopeful, at this stage, if the clothes he was wearing actually fitted. However, he looked like he had got up that morning and dressed in his smaller brother's clothes by mistake.

He measured waist, leg, chest, feet and arms. Interestingly he failed to take any notes during this painfully long measurement process. This was a fact that should have rung alarm bells.

After lunch a long, sleep inducing, briefing was under way. This covered how the apprenticeship would span the many different engineering roles. How it would move us towards the best fit for a future career etc. This briefing, however, singularly failed to mention that actual work was not much of a requirement.

It then droned on about the 'block release' college courses that we would have to enjoy. That woke me up with a bit of a shock. It was now clear that I was expected to go back to school for four weeks at a time. And undertake examinations in telecommunications, and pass them! Second thoughts were creeping in again.

The day then wound up with another sales pitch.

This time it was a book salesman. His pitch was for the two large volumes, and I mean large, of *'Telephony, Volumes 1 & 2 by Atkinson'*. These two tomes would definitely be needed for the college courses. They would be a source of knowledge for the work in telephone exchanges. They would open the doors for future promotions and generally be the panacea for all ills. And, importantly, could be paid for weekly by deductions from pay.

By now, of course, we were well beaten down and even the price of £6.25 (about our first week's wages!) didn't stop us. We all reluctantly signed the proffered document. As before this gave permission for the appropriate amount to be deducted directly from our diminishing weekly pay. His job done, like Brian, he disappeared.

I was beginning to wonder, at this stage, if I would have any actual pay left! Was there going to be anyone else walk in and sell us an essential item to haemorrhage some more cash from our hands!

Looking back now it was a form of blackmail or bullying. This was just to get sign-up for deductions from pay on those young innocent's first day! Given a bit of advice from the old lags we would not have signed for either. The sales guy, in particular, must have been making a bomb from the apprentices across the whole of London and beyond.

Those books, by the way, were never opened during 4 years of various college courses. They were never opened during a varied career in Telecommunications spanning 35 years. And have never been opened since retirement. Tell a lie; I did have a look inside the other day to see how much they had cost!

As a parting shot we were all given the address of our next GPO experience and sent home. My first destination was a place called Stamford Hill Automatic Telephone Exchange. This was to become a place that would feature strongly in my life for nearly 10 years.

CHAPTER 4-The Exchange, Grades and Hats

Stamford Hill Automatic Telephone Exchange; which we will hereafter call the Hill, was a large, dark daunting building. It was officially opened in 1934 to house the ever expanding network of telephone exchanges across London. It was very typical of the era, and would have been recognised immediately by any UK engineer for what it was.

The entrance to this imposing site was by very large oak double doors. Over the doors the words 'Telephone Exchange', set in concrete, proudly announced its true purpose. As you entered you were immediately confronted by another set of heavy, swinging double doors. On one of these an enamel sign read:

APPARATUS ROOM

PRIVATE

PLEASE WIPE YOUR BOOTS

I can quote this sign verbatim as I still have it. It hangs on the wall of my workshop at home!

Now a quick layout will help with the forthcoming pranks, larks and general mayhem. The ground floor housed a quite room, where you could go for a read, smoke, etc. Then there were some offices for external engineers. In addition you would find the vast battery room, the huge stand-by generators, some storage areas, a locker room, the first aid room and finally some toilets.

The first floor contained a small store room, the test room (basically a line of switchboards that could test external lines. In those days you could simply dial ENG and you would appear on this board), the Assistant Executive Engineer's office and masses of electro-mechanical Strowger equipment.

I will not bore you with the Strowger stuff. Sufficient to say it provided a step-by-step switching system to progress a call from one subscriber to another through the exchange. Each switch was large, heavy and dated. When I arrived most of the equipment had been successfully running there for over 30 years!

If you feel the need to learn more about Strowger I can recommend *'Telephony - Volumes 1 & 2 by Atkinson'* I can sell you a copy if you want!

Finally, on this floor, you would find very large Main and Intermediate Distribution Frames. These frames were about 30 metres long, about 8 shelves high and contained hundreds of thousands of copper wires called jumpers; plus 30 years of dust. The jumpers basically connected external subscribers through the frames to the necessary equipment for both incoming and outgoing calls.

The second floor housed masses more Strowger equipment and the third floor housed the canteen and switchboard room; with our 'Directory Enquiries' telephonists. These telephonists were the main focus of attention for some of the guys.

Finally there was a basement where you could find the boiler room and our 'unofficial' coffee room. You could also find the entrance to the cable chamber. This will feature in some surprising developments later.

The whole place was a mass of light-straw and battleship grey colours. These being the colours of the Strowger switch covers. It also had a particular smell. It is really hard to describe it. Try to think of 33 years of electro-mechanical devices bashing away in a closed building. Add the essence of the switch lubricant, Oildag. Mix this with 33 years of over-waxed wood parquet flooring and stir in some sweat and dust. If you can think of it like that, you're almost there.

All you need to do now is add the noise. Each type of switch made its own unique chatter as it moved the call on. Thousands of switches make a huge chatter! And, while walking between some racks of equipment, this could be deafening. Of course, this was before 'Health and Safety' thus the decibels were ignored. Many exchange engineers later suffered from tinnitus caused by this racket.

This was the sight and sound that was to present itself as I walked up through the main doors. My introductory note mentioned Stan as my contact, and on quietly enquiring to the first face encountered, I was ushered up to the test room.

Stan was the Technical Officer with Allowance or TOA as we shall now call it. Here you could find technicians (T2A), technical officers (TOs), a TOA and an Assistant Executive Engineer (AEE). Confused? Well how the hell do you think I felt! I, by the way was a TTA, Trainee Technician Apprentice!

Basically you started off life as a technician. You then progressed by age, experience and college examinations to Technical Officer and finally you could run the exchange as TOA. The AEE was the management grade responsible for the whole telephone exchange, but in reality the TOA ruled.

I was bemused when I was later told that all this was once defined by hats. In the 30s/40s the lower echelons went bareheaded. On promotion to TO you traditionally wore a flat cap. And, as a final badge of distinction, the TOA proudly wore a bowler!

Of course, as a very lowly apprentice and being on the lookout for a joke, this prompted me to buy a bowler from a junk shop (they are called charity shops now I believe). With which I proudly went to work. Unfortunately, someone had spotted me buying the aforementioned headgear, guessed what I was doing, and had passed the word to the lads before I arrived.

Nobody looked at my head or the hat. Nobody mentioned it or even gave me a second glance. Walking into the canteen wearing it created a zero response. Even the telephonists saw nothing. I later left the building rather crestfallen. I had thought it would at least cause some laughter. I was actually right. It did; after I had left!

Stan seemed to be an okay guy and welcomed me to the Hill. He gave me a quick guided tour; totally confusing everything with a bombardment of GPO 'speak' and three letter abbreviations along the way. There seemed to be about 30 or so engineers in the exchange, and all looked busy. Of course, that was because Stan was wandering around!

Dressed in the remnants of a once well tailored suit, he continually rolled his own cigarettes as we went. He never actually smoked any of these. They were just popped into various pockets for later consumption. When I say well tailored suit, by the way, I didn't mean actually tailored for Stan!

He decided to give me a notebook (GPO in large red letters on the front) as a good idea for me to note all I learned during those early days. He reversed this decision a few weeks later when perusal of the notebook revealed what I was actually learning!

I was then handed over to Arthur for my first training experience. Now Arthur was an old hand who remained one of the few TOs who actually did anything at the Hill. He maintained Strowger switches.

He was also one of the only engineers who still wore the traditional GPO dustcoat. This brownish, lightweight coat was an essential item to keep your clothes dust and Oildag free. However, it was dated and made you look like a warehouse worker. The young guys hated them.

The dustcoat was a full length design with a stylish ventilation slit half way up the back. However, this slit was the target for pranks. Creeping up behind the unsuspecting owner, the slit would be pulled apart, ripping it up the back to the neckline. As a result it was quite normal to see engineers in the exchanges wearing dustcoats with the slit firmly stitched up! I saw one guy, in Tottenham exchange, walking about with *'Don't You Fucking Dare'* neatly written above the offending design faux pas.

My dustcoat went the way of the overcoat, helmet and boots. They were stored from house to house for decades until my wife finally could bear them no longer. They ended up, unused, in a charity shop.

Now Arthur coveted his Strowger switches, he loved them, and he cleaned them. And, when he went on leave, he worried about them. During that first week he convinced me that each switch cover was highly pressurised thus cannot be touched. This was bollocks, of course; he just could not risk me poking my finger into his beloved equipment.

So, I followed him round watching and learning. At the same time watching and learning that nobody else seemed to be doing much at all. It was all breakfast break, official tea break, illegal morning coffee break, lunch break, afternoon tea break, afternoon illegal coffee break all interspersed with many quick cigarette breaks. I had never played so much snooker, cards and smoked so many cigarettes in my life. It was hard to keep up.

It was becoming clear that this ageing equipment functioned far better when left alone. However, a quote from the guidance on Strowger clearly stated;

> *'Continuous Strowger equipment maintenance is most important. Faulty equipment causes deterioration of service!'*

The reality, however, was the message given by the guys on every section,

"DON'T TOUCH ANYTHING!!!"

The routine maintenance, called 'routines' were seldom completed by the younger engineers and mostly just touched upon; reluctantly. We needed something important left to do for overtime you see!

Later in the apprenticeship I was given the opportunity to be 'let loose' on these switch routines. I rushed from one switch to the next, up and down ladders, cleaning, adjusting, removing, replacing and testing. The section TO calmly enquired,

"What the fuck are you doing?"

"The routines," I replied.

"You twat! Carry on like that and there will be nothing left for overtime!" he kindly observed.

The other thing difficult about this work was getting use to the noise. In between some of the loudest racks of equipment the old guys would not shout, they just mouthed the words. I really could not understand this 'communication' but they all did; and bizarrely continued elsewhere.

This could be across the canteen, on other sides of

a street or across the yard. Whole conversations would be had without speaking a word. I questioned this once in the canteen, as Arthur and Stan were silently debating something from different tables. All I got was puzzled looks, they didn't even realise they were doing it!

CHAPTER 5-Work Clothes, Tools and The Boss

At the end of that week word came through that I had work clothes and tool bags waiting for me in the stores. This also seemed a good time for me to be 'tooled up'; That is to say, provided with some real work tools. So, off I went to the stores.

The first shock was the size of the clothing so carefully measured during the first day. Everything was too big. And, I mean really too big. I stood there looking like a small child trying on his dad's overcoat. It actually didn't really matter though as I never used any of this stuff anyway.

Then the next shock was the amount of tools required for this job. A large green metal toolbox came with the large brown 'Gladstone' tool bag. This was added to by a large leather tool wallet plus a small leather tool wallet.

Into these poured screwdrivers, soldering irons, wire cutters, pliers, Buttinski (I will explain this one later); eye shields, solder wire and what seemed like hundreds of intricate Strowger adjustment tools. Weighed down with all this, wearing a large dustcoat, I struggled back twice across the yard to my designated locker to unload.

This was all a bit strange as most of the engineers seemed to do everything with just two tools. Long nosed pliers called '81s' and a screwdriver! All else was investigated and cleared using the 'Strowger Drop Test'.

This highly scientific, technical and complicated test necessitated the engineer to hold the faulty Strowger switch at waist height. He then dropped it on the floor! The resultant 'crash' cleared any dust causing a problem with internal relays, and often did the trick. It speaks volumes for the robustness of this old equipment that it still chugged along regardless.

The following is an interesting example as to how archaic everything was in the GPO. The wiring pliers, 81s, actually got their name in 1900 from the National Telephone Company where they were listed as Tool No. 81. This bore no resemblance to any modern stores numbering system, and the pliers bore no number 81 marked anywhere.

Nobody I ever asked could tell me why they were

called 81s; nobody knew why, they just were! Even more bizarre, during a recent visit by a young BT engineer to connect up broadband in my house. He spotted my long nose pliers on the shelf,

"Ah! 81s," he said!

By the end of second week with Arthur I was becoming well accustomed to the general daily routine at the Hill. And I was beginning to enjoy myself. This was a place where the emphasis was on smoking cigarettes, drinking tea, playing cards and pulling stunts. I could live with that.

Stan approached one morning and told me it was time to finally meet the AEE, Bernie. I had not even seen him at this stage and it soon became clear why.

Bernie was quite a character. In his 50s, tall, rather regimented with a trimmed moustache. When actually seen he always had a document in his hand looking very concerned and important. In later years, when I knew him well, he let on that there was never anything on the document,

"It keeps the guys on their toes," he explained.

He constantly smoked a very smelly pipe and the fog in his office was hard at times to see through. He reminisced continually about the war in the desert and revered Montgomery at every opportunity. He also proved to be a bit of a racist as everything wrong in the desert was the fault of 'bloody Arabs'. This he also extended to all ills with society everywhere. Now, before my Arab friends take offence, let's be clear, by Arabs Bernie actually meant anyone not English. Thus most of the planet!

Bernie was an entrepreneur. One of many that existed in the GPO system, and he basically used the Hill for his office with free telephone calls. His real purpose in life was selling and delivering electrical goods using his huge red estate car. This obviously was nicknamed the fire engine! Everyone knew about his sales 'career', nobody seemed to care; it was as it was.

This introduction to Bernie was short and to the point,

"What did your dad do during the war?" he opened.

"Er! I think he drove a tank," I responded.

"In the desert?" he enquired.

"No, in France," I remembered.

"Shame, shame...Oh well! Best get on then."

And with that my introduction to the man running the Hill was over.

Another of these illicit entrepreneurs surfaced a few years later. A friend had asked me to help advertise the first ever London beer festival at Alexandria Palace, and thus I was introduced to Jimmy. He was a TO in central London and ran an advertising agency from an empty room in the exchange.

Like Bernie, this was his office with free telephone calls. This was by no means a small event. Jimmy had hired an ancient open top London bus and about 10 of us were to ride on board dressed in 1920's costumes. A jazz band joined the group on the bus and a mass of advertising flyers were to be passed on to unsuspecting London shoppers.

The day was great fun and I remember surprising Michel Caine as he exited a London hotel heading for a taxi. I rushed up with papers in my grasp. He reached for his pen expecting a request for an autograph. Instead I pushed some flyers into his hand with a,

"Here Mike, hand a few of these out will you?"

He looked rather miffed. However, the very attractive lady by his side seemed well amused.

Looking back now it seems almost impossible that someone could organise all this illegally from a government building, and get away with it!

Well Bernie got away with it, and more. It was quite the norm for him to request a hand with heavy white goods when delivering; and I was dragged off several times to do my bit. On these occasions he would bleat on about the war, Arabs and his fading libido. He seemed to believe that these were all related in some way and used us for a sounding board.

Bernie, you see, had a mistress; a mistress that was quite demanding apparently. And they were demands that Bernie was beginning to fall short on.

John, one of the senior TOs, came up with the

solution one tea break. Bernie had joined us there for once, and was again regaling his woes. John mentioned that near to the London GPO training school 'Paul Street' was a sex shop. What Bernie needed was a dildo! Ben, a young black guy having recently joined us as a T2A, was on his way there for a course. So, Bernie immediately put in his order.

A week later Ben returned from his course. He placed a brown paper package on Bernie's desk and left with a big grin. A day or so later Bernie reappeared from his deliveries and carefully unwrapped his parcel. The contents dropped on to his desk with a thud and Bernie stepped back with a gasp. Ben had bought him a black one!

The laughter from every floor of the building could be heard three streets away.

It was now getting cold on that ride to the Hill and that could only mean one thing. Winter and the paraffin round were coming. I had a lot of catching up to do with George and told him all about my new job.

On that first weekend with the paraffin round, it was nice to climb back in the tanker again.

However, it really was beginning to look a bit fragile. George was his usual chirpy, cockney self and seemed pleased that I had got a job with the GPO.

"So, you're going to be riding those little red motorbikes around?" he asked.

"No mate, that's telegram boys. I'm joining the exchange telephone engineers," I replied.

"What! Sitting indoors with a phone stuck in your ear?" he exclaimed.

I tried to explain the many roles undertaken by those valiant folk but he really didn't get it. For him, anyone working indoors was dead from the neck up.

As it was the first time out we did a quick check round the lorry. Yep, the tyres were still worn out, and yes the brakes were on their last legs. The big taps at the rear, for dispensing the two coloured oils, were dripping and the huge brass tap spanners were still a bit loose. So, all still okay there then.

George was a bit preoccupied on the trip out from the depot. Word had got round that someone was pinching customers by driving around the area with a rogue lorry. This was not good news. This would not end well.

On about the second road of our delivery round, as we pulled around the corner, there they were. In front of us a lorry, even more decrepit than ours, was serving a group of houses; our houses,

"Stay here," commanded George, as he leapt out of the cabin.

Now, I am not one for taking commands very well, but these guys didn't look too friendly. So, on this occasion, I decided to comply with his request.

George walked straight up to the two protagonists and a heated debate began. Strangely, it was the two guys who were looking worried. In fact, the more the debate went on the more worried they became. Finally they both jumped in their lorry and sped off.

"What happened?" I asked.

"I warned them that big John from the depot was out with his boys looking for them. Apparently the boys are going to smash their kneecaps with paraffin tap spanners!" he calmly replied.

"Who is big John?" I puzzled.

"I don't know," said George with a wink, "he doesn't exist!"

It suddenly dawned on me that George had solved our problem without a blow being struck and I smiled at his audacity. Looking across the cabin he said,

"Look matey, always remember, if you need to tell a lie tell a big one!"

I would like to think that a future occurrence was unconnected, but some time later I heard that this pair were caught doing the same on a patch in Stepney and ended up in hospital!

CHAPTER 6-Jumpers, Siesta and Slack-Back

My time with Arthur was drawing to a close and Stan thought it a good idea for me to spend some time with Sid on the Main Distribution Frame, or MDF as we shall call it. As mentioned before these frames housed countless thousands of wires, called jumpers, most of which had been laying there for decades. Access to the shelves was aided by ladders that ran freely along the outside of the frame by way of an overhead rail.

When a new telephone line was to be connected, another wire was run on the MDF. The real problem was that old, redundant wires were seldom removed. Thus the whole thing was creaking under the weight of redundancy. The age of some of these wires was also reflected by the amount of dust scattered along the shelves. You could not work on this thing without getting covered.

I helped Sid run a few jumpers and then was told it was time to do something on my own; pull out an unwanted jumper wire. He showed me the connection of one side, cut it and suggested that I go to the location of the other end. This was to be found on the other side of the MDF and was identified by a unique number. The plan here clearly was to cut the other end, and pull the offending jumper out.

What I did not know was that the uniquely identified 'other end' had been connected to a reel of jumper wire containing about 200 metres of the stuff.

So, I innocently cut the wire and began to pull it through. I pulled and pulled and more and more jumper wire began to pile up around my feet. After a few minutes of this I was becoming buried in the stuff and began to smell a rat. On returning back to the original side to investigate, I found Sid and a few other technicians carefully watching a stopwatch. Bets had been taken on how long I would pull before giving up!

This prank was typical of those continually being pulled on the new apprentices. Luckily, for me, several years of George and the paraffin round had taught me much. I was hard to catch out and always dreamt up something more wicked in retaliation to their attempts. So, I was often bypassed and easier targets chosen.

Some of these TTAs were very green. They would happily be sent down to the local hardware store for a box of washer holes or a bag of disconnections. The guy running the shop would give them an empty bag to bring back!

Their other trial was the 'initiation'. For many years new apprentices had to undergo this ceremony mid-way through their three years. It was supposed to be a 'right of passage'; their acceptance by the other engineers. It normally took the form of being tied up with jumper wire and left in the female toilet. There they would stay, suffering giggles from passing telephonists, until the head supervisor found them. There would follow an abrupt, heated call to Stan and we would rescue the victim.

As I neared my time for this happy occasion I was given a reprieve. I was loaned to Edmonton exchange to cover some sickness and took my chance. When I arrived at Edmonton I made them laugh, telling of my initiation woes at the Hill. In unison they agreed that I was lucky, they would have been tougher. On my return to the Hill I made them laugh at my initiation woes at Edmonton. In unison they all agreed that I was lucky, they would have been tougher! Somehow these fabrications of the truth worked and I bypassed the ritual.

The jumper running I had experienced with Sid was a continual chore for all the guys at the Hill. It was often undertaken in pairs for ease, one person on each side of the MDF. As one person managed the jumper reel on one side the other waltzed the wire along the shelf, using the moving ladder, on the other.

Now, having found the location on the other side, and ensuring that sufficient wire had run through for the connection; a call of 'SLACK-BACK' was shouted. On this command the guy with the reel would cut his end of the wire and begin to connect.

Imagine if you will two guys enduring a day of this boring job. Then at every other jumper run, when half the wire had been pulled through, someone else not involved shouts, 'Slack-Back!' The wire is cut, and a connection is starting at the reel end. At the other side his partner is left with half a jumper, too short for anything.

"Fucking bastards!" would often be heard echoing as this work was interrupted. The joke wearing thinner as the day progressed.

Poor Graham was a constant victim. A gangly youth with very long hair, he looked like an advertisement for the Woodstock festival! His 'ban the bomb' badge continually irritated Bernie, who would berate him with,

"We didn't whip Rommel by banning the bomb you twat!"

Perpetually pulling jumpers, his mind was always somewhere else. And he was continually slightly muddled by 'wacky baccy'. Thus the 'Slack-Back' joke always worked. He seemed to spend half his life shouting *'fucking bastards.'* He will, much later, feature in a surprising final encounter.

It was about this time, while nosing in the small first floor store room, that I came across the platinum. There, sitting covered in dust, were two small jars. One labelled platinum contacts, the other platinum scrap. These tiny little worn contact scraps had been changed from Strowger switches for 30 years, and accumulated in the jar. That was the process, and in the past it had rigidly been stuck to.

I questioned Sid about this find and he was surprised they were still there,

"We never change those contacts any more." he

explained, "It's too much hassle. We just change the whole relay!"

"So why are the jars there?" I asked.

"Well, I guess one day someone will sell the platinum for scrap," he responded, eyes now lighting up!

I forgot all about those contacts until a few years later. Looking for something else, I noticed the jars still on the shelf. Picking up the now 'dust free' scrap jar, and peering inside, it was obvious someone had been busy.

The scrap platinum contacts had been replaced by solder clippings! The weight was about right, the colour was about right but solder was worthless. Several ounces of platinum scrap must have been worth hundreds of pounds! I can't think who could have done such a thing!

I would have loved to have been in the room when someone, from the de-commissioned Strowger exchange, found those jars. Then, they would be breaking the speed limit to rush to the nearest scrap metal dealer to cash in worthless solder scraps!

The MDF along with all the other racks in the exchange were adorned with letters and numbers. These were for identification or simply numbering. Now, this being the GPO these signs were not printed, they were slowly and carefully hand painted. And we had our own special sign writer for the exchanges in North Area Telephones.

His name was Billy and he defied all your images of what a sign writer should be. Standing about 5 feet 2 inches he needed a ladder for everything, even doors. He was left handed which caused most of his artwork to lean to the left; like a reversed italic. And he couldn't spell! Words like CLOSD or SMOKNG would appear on doors throughout the building. No one seemed to care about this; they just assumed it was GPO mnemonics!

You would often see new arrivals leaning slightly to the left trying to read his handiwork. Then after some head scratching, a Eureka moment would arrive as all fell into place. This was not restricted to the Hill; most of the north of London exchanges had been corrupted by his graffiti. I asked him once where he had learned his sign writing skills,

"The Borough Council," he said, "I used to write traffic signs!"

Another excellent use for the MDF was lunchtime siestas. It was warm up there. It was dark. And, more importantly, nobody could see you. A carefully placed blanket, stolen from the first aid room, shielded the incumbent sleeper from the layers of dust, and off they went into the land of nod! What would happen if someone actually needed the blanket in the first aid room was never considered.

One of the TOs, John, was always there and seemed able to drift off; even through the continual noisy chatter from Strowger switches.

Unfortunately this was not always well timed and a few months after my arrival, as the new boy, I was called by Bernie to meet the Executive Engineer. (Sorry, yet another grade, this time EE) Now, the EE was like a distant God to some of those guys. He seemed, to them, to be a mysterious character who wielded great power, made hugely important decisions and lived somewhere in an ivory tower. The reality was that he was a dick head.

He knew nothing about the exchange, nothing about the work undertaken there and actually wasn't that interested. He sort of appeared once every six months just to be seen.

This impromptu visit had been caused by some concern, higher up the managerial tree, over the exchange statistics. I guess if the Hill's performance was dropping, someone must have touched something! In truth, as an aside, certain switches were knowingly used to record and check exchange performance. These switches miraculously were always maintained to perfection, cleaned and observed by the guys at the Hill.

The EE duly, without any interest, shook my hand while looking directly over my shoulder. The handshake was of the limp variety that makes you want to wipe your hand down the back of your trousers afterwards. Bernie, noting my discomfort, gave me a wink and led the EE along the MDF discussing the wonderful attributes of his engineers as he went.

Just at that moment loud snores could clearly be heard coming from the top shelf of the frame. A puzzled look on the EE's face was mirrored by a bead of perspiration appearing on Bernie's. I stood rooted to the spot trying not to be there!

Now here was a lesson for the future. Sometimes ignorance is bliss and doing nothing can be the best policy. The EE had no knowledge of the working life of an exchange. He therefore did not want to enquire about a noise that may make him look stupid. So, he ignored it as though it was a 'normal occurrence in a Strowger exchange'.

Bernie, on the other hand, knew damn well what the noise was. He also knew damn well who was making it. However, exposing one of his engineers (you know, the ones with wonderful attributes!) as sleeping on the job, was not a possibility. So, he ignored it as though it was a 'normal occurrence in a Strowger exchange!'

The uneducated questions from the EE being over, and Bernie's baffling, indecipherable responses being completed, the EE was gently led by the arm away from the scene.

Bernie caught up with me later that day,

"Just like the army my boy, bullshit baffles brains! Don't forget that," he said.

I never did.

CHAPTER 7-Derek's Eggs and Paddy's Brains

A few months into my GPO experience it was time for me to join the external engineers for a few weeks. Here I would learn the mysteries of telephone installations, repairs and updates. This would be my education into cable laying, repairs and removals. It would provide an opportunity for me to climb poles and descend holes. Well, that's what it was supposed to be. In actual fact it became another wander through the rituals of scams, jokes and general mayhem.

Morning breakfast was a ritual not just reserved for the guys in the exchange. The external engineers also enjoyed the privilege. They would leave the yard in unison with their mid-bronze green vans, and descend on the local cafe. Normally this cafe would be chosen for being out of sight. Here they would stay for about 40 minutes chatting and eating their breakfast.

When I joined this happy bunch I was rather staggered by their lack of productivity. And this, coming from one now experienced in telephone exchange activities, speaks volumes. On arriving at the cafe they would casually pull out the paper, check the racing or football pages, search for tits and then banter. But never once was work mentioned. I sat with them with no idea as to where we were going or what we were going to do. Then suddenly, in unison, we all got up and left.

The vans disappeared in varying direction to tackle the day's jobs. They generally did as little as possible with, like the exchange, a small number of guys appearing to keep the telephone lines running.

Round about 11.30am I would be told to 'bugger off' and to get back at 2.00pm. They would then disappear for lunch somewhere. Quite often, on returning to meet up with the guys, they would tell me to sod off home as there was not much on! Regardless of how much work was on, and regardless of how difficult or easy it was.

The unwritten rule was to complete a maximum of 3 faults a day. Once that had been accomplished they disappeared like snowflakes in the sunshine; only to miraculously reappear at 5.00pm to park up the vans in the yard again.

One guy, Derek, continually amused me with his choice of breakfast, always the same. Two slices of toast with two fried eggs; then all covered in pepper and soaked in vinegar. This was washed down with a large mug of tea. He often dared me to try this delicacy for myself. I did once; never again!

He was a very large guy. And he was always red in a face which he continually tapped with a handkerchief. This was whipped, like magic, from his jacket pocket. Rumour had it that he would often get wedged into manholes and need rescuing. This, he explained, was due to government cutbacks reducing the size of manhole covers!

Whilst these guys were fun to be with, and full of stunts, they were not all particularly blessed with intelligence. Once I was helping Derek to replace a faulty wire running through a conduit (this being like a long length of clay drain pipe). This faulty wire led to some subscribers houses. I watched in awe as he cut the faulty wire at both ends of the conduit. Then he casually pulled it out.

He then attempted to push a new length of wire up the conduit towards the houses. This of course was impossible as it kept snagging, bending and refusing to budge. His solution was to try again with a thick piece of overhead cable. This with the intention of attaching the new telephone wire to the exposed end of the overhead cable, and pull them both through the conduit.

This also failed due to bends in the conduit run and general overcrowding. All this was being attempted while sitting half way down a GPO manhole; not the easiest of manoeuvres.

At this stage I could hold back no longer,

"Why didn't you attach a new wire to the old one before pulling it out, and use the old wire to pull the new one through?" I asked.

His face went from confusion to deep concentration then enlightenment,

"Because we always do it like this! Anyway it's too fucking late now isn't it?" he replied.

More grunting continued as he pulled and pushed the cable again. Following on from my previous, bloody obvious, observation I added,

"Er no, there are about six pairs of wires going from this manhole to the houses. Why not cut one of them and pull two new ones through?"

This time I think the suggestion was getting a bit too complex for Derek. But after some thought he came up with a much better solution,

"No need to pull through two as we can cut one of the redundant wires to pull through the new one!" he countered.

"What do you mean redundant wires?" I asked, now becoming somewhat confused myself.

"Well, some of these wires are not being used," he responded.

By now I was beginning to question my own understanding of life, the universe and everything.

"Are you telling me that some of these wires are not being used?" I questioned.

"Yes, of course. We never use them all do we?" he explained.

"Well, why don't we just use one of the existing unused wires to replace the faulty one that you have just pulled out?" I pondered aloud.

To give him his due, instead of calling me smart arse, he agreed that this might actually be a good idea. We quickly connected both ends of the aforementioned 'redundant' wire and cleared the fault.

Being just a youngster, I felt a bit uneasy about the exposure of Derek's somewhat limited lateral thinking. So, I asked him if it was all right for me to ask lots of questions. He replied,

"Yes matey, you're here to learn ain't ya!"

One thing he did warn me about though, was to be wary of the exchange engineers. They are all thick and don't know anything, he would preach. They are all lazy and never do anything, he would moan. All they think about is drinking tea and messing about, he observed. Little did he know that, before embarking on this external adventure, the guys in the exchange had warned me the same word for word about them!

Of course, back at the exchange, we interacted and liaised all the time with the multitude of external folk. There was testing to be done, stories to swap and the usual banter that comes from two seemingly rival groups.

As I had the opportunity to join both these sides from time to time; I was happily neutral. This was part and parcel of the apprenticeship programme.

It was always interesting when everyone joined together in the canteen to swap stories. These guys could be incredibly intelligent or incredibly dumb but all were characters worth listening to.

Paddy the engineer was my favourite. He continually looked like a cartoon character. His 4 foot 8 inch frame was dressed in rough dungarees and a battered tweed jacket. A pork-pie hat and boots 3 sizes too big completed the picture. His face and hands always looked as though he'd been cleaning a chimney. This was the site that greeted the subscriber at the door; either to install a new phone or, heaven forbid, to repair a fault.

Various bosses had historically tried to dress him in the standard GPO issue clothing but he always metamorphosed back into his favourite attire. I guess today you would call it branding!

His inability to connect, repair or install anything to do with telephony was legendary. In fact today you would not have let him hold a screwdriver let alone try to connect anything. Yet, there he was, let loose among our valued subscribers. To complicate matters further his strong Irish brogue made it almost impossible to understand anything he said!

Reports would come back through the canteen whenever someone had had to rescue a subscriber from his disastrous adventures. And, whilst some of these tales were apocryphal or actually really attributed to others, I am sure many were true. I can recall a few of the classics but it would take a stand alone book to recount them all.

It was quite early one morning when an irate subscriber dialled ENG and screamed down the phone that one of our engineers had destroyed his grand piano. Grand Piano! (a WTF moment). After a quick call to the downstairs external team office, an engineer was quickly dispatched to the complainant's home. The poor engineer in question had unfortunately popped in to waste some time and had been cornered. He was sent off to discover the cause of the problem.

Apparently, Paddy had called there early in the morning to connect a new phone. Now to educate the non technical amongst you; telephone wire, once installed and run inside the house, is connected to a small plastic box called a block terminal. The telephone itself connects to this block terminal via a cable from the back of the phone.

Normally the block terminal was screwed to the wooden skirting board near the floor or on any other suitable unsighted surface. It makes sense, of course, to fit the block terminal near to where the phone is to be sighted.

So, on this occasion, when asked as to where he might like the phone placed, the subscriber unfortunately told Paddy "near the piano". Some time later, after saying goodbye to a departing Paddy, the subscriber casually wandered into his living room to peruse his new phone.

Paddy had pushed the telephone wire underneath the carpet, poked a small hole in the carpet and pulled the wire up towards the piano. Next he had screwed the block terminal to the piano leg with one inch screws. Finally connecting the telephone to the block terminal and placing it on the piano, conveniently near the keyboard.

I do not know how much this cost to put right but I think the guy got free phone calls for life. Paddy's defence was that he had merely done what the subscriber had asked for!

On another occasion one of the better equipped external engineers, i.e. he actually new what he was doing, was called out to help Paddy. It would appear that Paddy had completed an installation but was having difficulty getting it to work. Now this time it was a more complex installation being a plan involving two lines plus extensions. Why on earth they would risk giving this job to Paddy is anyone's guess.

Now again, for the uninitiated, some of the more complex installations need an earth wire. This wire was somewhat similar to the earth wire in the household electricity system. The normal and best solution for this requirement was to connect a wire to a cold water pipe via a clamp. The cold water pipe, of course, was connected directly through to the earth via incoming water supply pipes. Otherwise an external earth spike was driven into the ground to make an earth connection.

On arriving, the engineer could find no fault with the installation, albeit completed in a less than professional manner. He began to scratch his head for a solution. Going back to basics he asked Paddy where he had connected the earth wire. Paddy explained that in running in the cables he had located a cold water pipe in the loft and connected it to that.

Thinking that a loose connection may be the culprit, the engineer climbed up into the loft to investigate.

He quickly found the problem. Paddy had groped about in the dark and, on feeling a cold water pipe, had rapped his earth wire several times around it. Unfortunately, the aforementioned cold water pipe was, in fact, a pram handle! Luckily the subscriber never learned about the faux pas and all was quickly tidied up and tested okay.

Perhaps a final parting shot was the error, to be fair, often made by new installation engineers. Paddy arrived at the subscriber's house to install a simple phone connection. He successfully ran his wire up to a window frame. Drilled a hole in the frame, and threaded the wire through. Pulling in enough wire for the connection from the inside; he wired up the block terminal, connected the phone, tested it and left.

Now, all ex-engineers know what's coming. Some time later the subscriber opened his window ripping the block terminal off the skirting board and landing the phone, with a thump, on the floor.

It was, in fact, a sash window and Paddy had passed his wire through the window and window frame. Thus, when the window moved so did the wire and by default everything attached to it!

It does beggar belief in this modern age of customer service, efficiency and professional training that these events could possibly happen. But, they did. More strangely to everyone today; nobody then really seemed to care.

I was back out on the paraffin round that weekend and business was hotting up. So were my learning experiences! At one house where there seemed to be a family in every room; I knocked on a door and was asked to come in. Now, these were a family that I had served many times before and knew well; however, not as well as I was about to.

On entering, I was met by a vision of the guy's arse pumping up and down on a groaning wife. In the corner a television blared which he intently watched. Whoever said that guys can't multi-task? Without altering his stride he turned his head and said,

"Hi Joe, the usual 5 gallons of blue mate."

Then he continued as if I was not there. The oilcan was by the door so I picked it up and beat a hasty retreat.

At the tanker I relayed this experience to George. Who, for the first time ever, seemed very keen to carry the filled can back. He did; but came back looking rather disappointed. He was too late for the show. I noted with some interest that, in the following weeks, he always rushed up to serve this house!

Looking back now I can understand how George always seemed flush with money. He made about 10p profit on every gallon we sold and we could empty the tanker and go for a refill on just one good Saturday. Whilst Saturday was the big day for deliveries, he did work on his own a few days through the week. So, although this was seasonal work, he must have been making over £150 per week when most ordinary folk were on about £20.

I am sure the tax man saw very little of it. That being said, he was very generous and always looked after his happy band of helpers. By the time I joined the GPO I was given £10 for a Saturday shift. Much more, I might add, than the GPO was paying apprentices for a full week! He also bought lunch, provided gallons of hot sweet coffee, dosed us with rum on freezing days, and educated us in the ways of the world. The sort of education that you can't get from parents!

In addition to this, Christmas tips were a very lucrative bonus. I do not know if it was the bad winter weather or just 'time of year' generosity but everyone gave something at Christmas. At the end of this particular Saturday I could be going home with £50 plus in tips. A nice little earner as they say!

The winter I started with the GPO it was bloody cold. Ice tested the best of drivers and a sprinkle of snow settled on the paraffin lorry windscreen. We had stopped for coffee and I stared out onto the wintry scene.

It made me ponder on the stability of a lorry with 1,000 gallons of paraffin skidding and crashing into something. The resultant inferno causing death and destruction, blazing fires leaking across the road setting houses and cars alight. People would be running in all directions, there would be panic and mayhem.

I thought of George heroically struggling with the wheel; pushing me clear in desperation to steer the lorry from the path of innocent bystanders. He would hang on in there to the last second to bravely save lives,

"What would you do if the lorry caught light and was out of control?" I casually enquired.

"Jump the fuck out," he responded.

"What about everyone else?" I pondered.

"Fuck them," he said, "You see, matey, heroes are normally dead people!"

Disappointing, but he did have a point.

It was after this coffee induced reality lesson that I was confronted but yet another reality; the perils of overcrowded houses using paraffin. As we turned into the next street a blackened ruin confronted us. Each window of our first customer's house was burned. The roof was gone and a strong smell of burning still clogged the senses. We jumped out of the lorry to survey the ruin. This was a 25 gallon plus house, thus a good customer for George. He was pissed off to say the least!

One of the former residents, a young West Indian guy, was stood, shell shocked, peering through the remains of the window,

"Anyone hurt?" enquired George, trying to look concerned.

"No, everyone got out," he said, "someone's fire blew up!" he added.

"Oh well! So long as everyone is all right," George replied, still trying to look concerned.

As we climbed back into the lorry his true colours emerged;

"Fucking idiots!" he complained, "that's going to cost me pounds this year!"

Well you can't blame him I suppose, but I left the road wondering about the quality of the paraffin we were selling. I also could not forget the happy, laughing families that I had seen here the week before. Where were they all now?

CHAPTER 8-Limping Store Men and Face Masks

Back at the Hill the following week Stan had some call up papers for me to attend my first TTA training course. This was to be at London's Paul Street and would be the first of many such courses throughout my career.

Now, here I will admit that the GPO, Post office and finally BT were very good at one thing. That was training people. Be it engineering, clerical, scientific, technical or occupational. It was all delivered in the best, sometimes most expensive, fashion.

The fundamental problem was not the quality of the training; it was the mindset of those attending. Their utter indifference to anything educational was legendary. These courses were assessed during the apprenticeship but afterwards mere 'attendance' was enough. So, at least for the TTAs, the results were important.

However, here was a problem to tax Stan. The course was a week away, so what could he get me to do in the interim? After my stint outside I was expecting him to say sod off home for the week. Or, of course, I could pop out with Bernie delivering fridges! But no, Stan had several ideas. Test room, Switchboard, Strowger equipment, jumpers. They were all processed, then, the Stores were muted.

The Stores at the Hill pretty much represented the standard for telephone exchanges across the country. Run by misfits, stocked with stuff dating back to 1934 and emanating an air of mystery.

To my mind it seemed that all stores staff had something wrong with them. It could be a missing leg, a mangled arm or damage between the ears. Unfortunately, for them, most of these deficiencies resulted from accidents at work. And, in true GPO fashion, a job for life meant just that. If you could no longer climb up poles or disappear down holes then it was the stores!

I remember one particular morning sat in the front of a GPO van. I was doing another stint with the installers and, as usual, not much was happening. My colleague Billy and I were idly reading newspapers while waiting for lunch. We were not eating anything as we had just left the coffee break cafe.

Wandering towards us, along the pavement, appeared a wizened figure. He was bent in the back, had an eye patch covering an unshaven face. He carried an arm hanging loose to the side; and one leg almost dragged along, propped by home-made walking stick.

"Fuck me," declared Billy, "are there any vacancies in the stores?"

William, the stores boss fascinated me; I could watch him for hours. He was very tall, skinny and lurched forward as though he was falling over at all times. He always carried the Times newspaper under his arm and rumour had it that he actually read it as well. As he propelled his frame across the yard he would continually talk to himself as if in heated debate. However if interrupted by a "hello Will" he could stop in mid flow, politely respond, and then lurch onwards again.

His whole demeanour was as if he was constantly searching for something in the distance. I once watched him complete the Times crossword while I was concentrating hard on smoking two fags, drinking a mug of tea and perusing a rather disgusting magazine. In my defence, the magazine was being passed round for educational purposes. Whether he actually put all the right words in the crossword I will never know. However I suspect he did.

It was with great delight, therefore, that I discovered that Stan's decision was for me to experience a week in the stores. Here was a chance to get to snoop around an 'off-limits' playground.

Picture for a moment the hundreds of different tools. Then the myriad of equipment parts, the telephones of every colour, and the cables of every dimension. Then the clothing, boots and everything you could think of to keep the GPO machine running. Finally all you have to do is imagine a thick layer of dust on everything, add a musty smell, and you are there.

What amazed me, after perusing most of the many shelves of stock, was how old some of the stuff was. Here you could find spare parts for candlestick telephones. Old style black Bakelite phones still in their boxes. Black ink, pen nibs and ink wells from the wartime. It really was an Aladdin's cave. If only eBay was around then. We could have cleaned up!

I was put under the guidance of Archie. A guy with one arm missing following an accident; this being amply compensated by the size of his heart. For some reason he always wore a suit; a badly fitting one at that. This was brightened by a bow tie that drew the eyes away from the empty sleeve. The sleeve in question was always pinned to his lapel by what looked like a nappy pin. The rumour was that the suit was his dad's demob suit. If this was true I hope it was a better fit on his dad.

Archie's co-patriot, Jim, had a terrible face disfigurement which nobody ever mentioned, and I never questioned. I assume that the GPO, in its wisdom, felt that Jim was better hidden out of sight. This empire, of course, was all managed by William.

I had a heart stopping moment with Jim's disfigurement some years later. I was clearing out some unused jumper wires from the top shelf of the main frame; much to the disgust of various engineers sleeping there. This was causing masses of dust to erupt, most of which I was inhaling. So, I decided to requisition a protective mask from the stores.

On arriving at the stores I found the usual crowd of external engineers hiding from the outside world. They would be there for hours. The guys would chat away while stretching the time-scales required for changing a screwdriver to the limit. Walking through the group I strode up to the counter and boldly said to Jim,

"Have you got a face mask?"

The immediate deadly silence was unhelpful as the inference of my words registered between my ears. Jaws dropped, eyes fell and I saw my life rushing past. Luckily for me, Jim was unfazed. With a twinkle in his one visible eye he said,

"I have, and it looks like you need it more than me!"

With much laughter ringing in my ears I took my mask and my reddening face quickly away.

Whilst at the stores, Archie filled me in with the background to the strange behaviour of William. It would appear that some years previously he had been a TO recognised as a hopeful for promotion to management. I don't think that this was solely due to reading the Times. I am sure there was more to it than that. Apparently everyone knew that he was destined for higher, greater things, and it was a certainty that he would fly.

However the stress and pressure that he endured, while preparing for the interview, finally told. In his mind he personally would let everyone down if he failed. It was big, very big; a lad from the bottom rung being propelled upwards. A day before the interview he suffered a mental breakdown and was never the same again. His sideways move to the stores was arranged and that was that. This was a lesson for me that I never forgot. Nothing is worth getting that stressed over.

At least, while fulfilling this one week obligation, I did manage to change some of my ill fitting work clothes. These quickly were swapped for ones that resembled normality. And I managed to extend my collection of never-to-be-used specialist Strowger tools. I also quickly discovered why there was so much stuff covered in dust. Stores folk just do not want to give you anything.

To these guys it was like giving away something that personally belongs to them. A typical conversation would go;

"I need a manhole cover lifter."

To which Archie responds, "Sorry, we haven't got any."

The engineer observes, "I can see one there on the shelf."

Archie counters with, "Yes, but that's the last one and someone might need it!"

Checkmate!

CHAPTER 9-Double Chins and Line Ups

The week in the stores over it was off to Paul Street. This was the 'A' course. The first of three courses for TTAs helpfully designated A, B, C

You have to imagine the excitement of this. Here I was being paid to travel into central London. It wasn't London itself that was novel. As a Stoke Newington kid I had been jumping on buses to roam the streets there for years. Times were different then. No, it was the fact that somebody was actually paying me to do it.

This first course was an introduction to some of the technical skills needed for the different roles in the GPO. You had to learn them all as, at this stage, where you would end up in the GPO system was unknown.

TTAs from all over the place descended on Paul Street and some of these faces I recognised from both the interview and the induction briefing.

One of these guys started the proceedings off well by larking around on the fire escape outside. He was jumping down the metal steps, feet together, and two steps at a time when his shoes got caught in the under-curve of the step. Why he was actually doing this is beyond me, however, it seemed funny at the time.

Unfortunately, as he fell helplessly forward, arms outstretched, the metal dug into the rear of both heels. This tore into his skin ripping part of both heels asunder.

I think we were more shocked than he was and luckily there was a rather excited first aider amongst the Paul Street staff. He was excited as this was the first time he had ever been called to a real incident! And he had rushed there like a man possessed to ensure he beat off any competition. However, he did overcome being out of breath and managed to stem the flow of blood.

The end result was our apprentice colleague rushed in an ambulance to the local hospital for stitching. He never returned to the course. And I never saw or heard of him again. One thing was for sure, his tap dancing days were over.

All of this first aid excitement, plus our experiences up to that time, were enthusiastically shared. And, all the events seemed similarly bizarre. This enthusiastic chatter did not help the lecturer draw our attention to the matters at hand. And his valiant struggles to gain our attention became desperate. Finally, he screamed.

"I'm your AEE!"

This declaration intended to shock us into obedience but somehow failed. The old lags had already fully explained how all AEEs were dick-heads.

I can remember him now, standing there getting redder and redder. He was, to put it bluntly, grossly fat. With this came the most amazing double chin, the likes of which I have never seen again. As he spoke it wobbled up and down like a balloon filled with water. It was very hard to concentrate on his wise words as I was transfixed on his chin. Looking around the room you could see all eyes moving up and down; a bit like the communal head movement at Wimbledon!

His lectures on theory were interspersed by sessions on practical work overseen by the Paul Street technical instructors. These guys were, for the most part, ex TOs from the London exchanges.

Thus, they had seen it all. Some were great guys and very helpful, some were unhelpful idiots.

On a later course we were each intently adjusting the contacts of a Strowger relay. To put you in the picture this could be a very tricky operation and concentration was a necessity. I was actually quite good at this and all was going well. At that moment a policeman walked in unannounced and wandered around the room.

He pointed 6 of us out, including me, and went on his way. You could cut the tension with a knife. What the hell was going on? One of the less helpful instructors; Gary, explained that the local nick needed us for an identity parade. And we 6 were the lucky chosen ones.

Now, I had heard many times rumours of corruption at Stoke Newington police station. This came from many sources and was assumed to be true. Evidence fabrication, racism, unprovoked violence, perjury, drug trafficking and bribery just to name a few of the lesser accusations.

At that time I assumed that all police followed this pattern. Thus I didn't want to volunteer for a line up. After all, I could end up being 'fixed up' for a crime I knew nothing about. These thoughts were given some credence years later when corruption at Stoke Newington police station was fully exposed. Operation 'Jackpot' tried to clean up the mess, policemen lost their jobs and the whole drugs squad was disbanded.

Anyway, I had nearly completed a complex relay adjustment, and was not even asked if I would mind going. Also this meant a lot; a fail could jeopardise my route to a job in the exchange. So I said no. This immediately pissed off Gary and he tried to persuade me to change my mind. In fact he rapidly became quite aggressive and resorted to blackmail tactics. What an arse. Basically if I did go, my relay might pass. If I didn't go, well, who knows!

This in turn pissed me off. And I looked him in the eye, asked him to concentrate and said no. He walked away, and the guy at the next table succinctly summed up the situation for me,

"You're fucked!" he kindly observed.

The remaining 5 'volunteers' happily wandered off to a waiting police van and the rest of us broke off for lunch. Gary's gaze was burning a hole in my back as we went. These volunteers returned from the 'nick' half way through lunch and appeared to have had a fun time. They were well looked after, thanked for their help and given a lift back.

When I got back to the workroom the fragile contacts on my relay were all bent at right angles! There also appeared to be an argument going on. One of the other instructors; Peter, had seen what had happened and was, rather heatedly, arguing my right of refusal.

Peter stormed up to my work table, picked up the mangled relay and loudly said,

"Yes, good work. That's a pass!"

At this Gary just went red and walked away. With that my relay adjustment course was complete and my contact with the relay mangler over.....That is, that's what I thought!

Years later, as a senior manager, I had occasion to visit Paul Street to question costs and viability for some up and coming international training via satellite. I recognised Gary immediately, I never forget a face. Incredibly he was now running the place and was clearly under a lot of pressure.

A meeting followed and, much to the surprise of my colleagues, I bombarded Gary with bloody awkward questions. I hit him with unanswerable problems and general made him sink perspiring into his seat.

It didn't make any difference to any decisions, of course, but I had a good time. As we left, one of my colleagues enquired,

"Bloody hell mate that was a bit harsh wasn't it?"

"Not really Dave, bit of history there pal!" I replied.

I think you call it Karma don't you?

As a final twist, double chin was there as well. Only, this time the chin was gone, so was the stomach and so was the rest of his body. It was a bit of a shock really. He was stick thin, fit and ageing well. At the meeting I mentioned to him, over some pink cake, that I had once sat some courses here.

"You wouldn't remember me," he said, "I was a bit fat!"

Some of the GPO training courses in those days were held at a little known establishment called Bletchley Park. Famous now, of course, but then not much was known about the place. I clearly remember hidden behind a blackboard announcing lunch menus a plaque. On the plaque there were some vague words about Bletchley and the Second World War. Nobody took any notice of it.

Today the name is immediately recognised as the birthplace of the computer and the breaking of the Enigma code. Alan Turing, quite rightly, is a famous name. However not much, if anything, is ever mentioned about Tommy Flowers.

Tommy had, before the war, worked on the possibility of the use of electronics for running telephone exchanges. He was convinced that an all electronic system was possible. This was undertaken at the GPO research establishment at Dollis Hill.

Little did he know then that this was leading to the first ever computer; Colossus. He was transferred to Bletchley Park in 1943 and got on well with Turing. However, the management were not convinced with his ideas. He ended up having to work very much on his own, and provide most of the funding himself!

However, Tommy's Colossus was successfully demonstrated in December 1943, and the rest is history as they say. Nice to think, as I tap away at my laptop, that a humble GPO engineer started it all.

As a 'thank you', and in recognition of the fact that Tommy had saved countless lives, ended the war early, invented the world's first computer and paid for all this out of his own pocket. The Government awarded him £1,000! If you are sat there assuming I have missed off a few noughts by mistake; unfortunately you are wrong.

Naturally I shared these 'training course' experiences with George during the following weekend paraffin round.

"You should have just waited for this Gary outside and head-butted him!" he sagely advised.

"Er, I would actually like to keep this job," I replied.

Well he had a point I suppose. His world seemed far simpler than mine. He was his own boss and didn't have anyone else to answer to. Except, obviously, the many 'bits on the side' that he continually juggled!

One thing I was realising though, after meeting so many new guys at work. George was a bit of a philosopher. His conversations were 180 degrees away from the ones at the exchange and did open my eyes a bit to the realities of real life outside.

One Saturday we munched on his favourite lunch. This was thick cut cheddar cheese sandwiches sprinkled with sliced pickled onions. These were washed down with the hot coffee delivered from an old battered vacuum flask. The sandwiches tasted vaguely of paraffin. In fact everything eaten in the cab tasted of paraffin. You just got used to it.

"You see this here vacuum flask?" he asked.

"Yes, what of it?" I mused.

"Well, it keeps hot stuff hot and cold stuff cold," he observed.

"Well?" I countered.

"Well, how the fuck does it know?" he concluded.

After a brief ponder he would come up with another gem,

"If girls are made of sugar and spice and all things nice," he questioned.

"Er! Yes," I said.

"Then how come they taste of anchovies?" he asked.

Hard to answer, naturally, so I didn't try. Instead I questioned his current lifestyle. How on earth he managed to keep several lady friends on the go at the same time.

"The trick is keep them all well apart, and most important; don't crap on your own doorstep!" he helpfully explained.

"On your own doorstep! Then what about Mrs Smith in the flat opposite yours? And that blonde bit round the back of the Gardens?" I questioned.

"Er! Well that's complicated," he replied, "you see matey, sometimes life is like a crap. You think you can control it, But when you've got to go, you've got to go!"

And with that he pulled his cap, plus wig, over his eyes and had a snooze!

I didn't quite understand this reasoning at the time. It was all a bit too deep. However, I think I do now! That was the quality of the strange philosophical observations that continued throughout the day!

George had not always lived a charmed life with the ladies. When he was young he had married a Gypsy girl who he had met at a fairground. They had a baby girl and shortly afterwards this 'love of his life' disappeared back to her Gypsy family. He was left to raise his daughter alone. He talked about it only once and still choked up as the memory came back.

I never did discover what he actually did during the summer. He always changed the subject. I suspect not a lot. Each year, as I gradually became more and more embroiled in the GPO world, I saw him less and less. Then, one summer, I moved away from Gibson Gardens and lost touch.

The last I heard of George he had bought his dream 'Bed and Breakfast' business in Bournemouth, and had retired there with one of his on/off girlfriends. What his customers made of his bawdy London reminiscences I will never know; but, I bet they came back for more.

CHAPTER 10-Requisition Mayhem and Swarfega

Quite often Stan had the temerity to take annual leave. Unfortunately for Stan this was the real stuff, not the scheduled sick variety. (All explained later) As the Technical Officer with Allowance he was outside of such advantages.

When he left us in the lurch like this, a stand-in was chosen. The 'chosen one' naturally did not take on this task for no additional pay. A covering allowance was duly paid.

Now, you have to understand that the allowance was not the real driver for covering this role. Among the older engineers in the exchange, this role was coveted. In days gone by it was the pinnacle of their hopes for promotion. Actual promotion into real management, from the lads, was not the done thing. Thus this role was undertaken for prestige.

The real proof of all this was the hard fact that the Technical Officer with Allowance did not do overtime. He dished it out, managed it and checked it; but while on allowance, didn't do it. Simple maths exposed this role as not a great money spinner; this in a world where overtime made such a big difference.

Now on this occasion Arthur took his turn in the chair. And he was well pleased. As the same age as Stan and similar experience, there was always a bit of jealousy. He would always 'lord it over' when covering for Stan. The signing-on book was red lined with relish, the signing-off book timed to the second and overtime planned with military precision. A blind eye was taken to all the scams; he was, after all, coming back to the fold quite quickly!

What he loved was to be seen to make a decision. And his chance quickly came. The fuel that powered the huge stand-by generators was low and needed to be replenished. The generators were started often to check working capability and drank fuel at an alarming rate. To that end a 500 gallon fuel tank was buried beneath the yard; an accident just waiting to happen.

Out came the requisition pad, boxes were ticked, urgency demanded and signatures flourished. Unfortunately Arthur had fallen short on a couple of interesting points. There was about 100 gallons already in the tank, thus not enough room for the 490 demanded. He had read 10 gallons remaining from the generator routine sheet; a supposed full stop being the missing nought.

He also had failed to notice that, alongside the term fuel on the requisition sheet, there were different choices! His tick did, in fact, indicate petrol as the requirement; a simple slip that normally would cause no problem. Except that the generators ran on diesel. Arthur, of course, knew this but was blissfully unaware of the error and the impending catastrophe.

The day of the delivery quickly came. It was after all an emergency. At least, it soon would be. The delivery fuel tanker was casually backing into the yard as Arthur hurried out with his requisition copy. As the Civil Service, this would necessitate several signings; and Arthur was not going to miss the glory. Anyway, Bernie was out delivering white goods so this was all his.

Off came the generator fuel manhole cover, and in went the pipe from the tanker. And, as it pumped away Arthur and the driver became completely engrossed in the complexities of triple signing procedures.

Most of us were casually watching this from the side window. It was nice to have something to break the monotony of listening in to other people's conversations, practising pull ups and generally waiting for the lunch break. As usual the exchange was being run by about two people and even they were not doing much!

Standing next to me, John casually remarked,

"Can you smell petrol?"

"Yes I can.", I replied, "so what?"

"Because that tank happens to hold diesel, that's why," he answered.

"Do you think we should mention it?" I said.

But, this was to an empty room. Everyone was gone. Windows were being flung open, shouts were made and the clatter of boots rushing down the stairs echoed up the through the doorway. Arthur...Petrol, PETROL!

By now about 401 gallons of Shell's finest petrol had been mixed with 100 gallons of ageing diesel and was beginning to overflow. The driver was quick to dash and turn off the pump but the damage had been done. Nobody seemed to move. An eerie silence now descended on the yard. Only the chatter of Strowger switches could be heard in the distance through open windows with gaping faces.

Arthur broke the spell by clearly and succinctly summing up the situation,

"Fuck!" he said.

"Fucking hell!" returned the combined chant.

What happened next was a once in a lifetime lesson in action in the face of adversity. Or, as I like to call it, how to get out of the shit without getting bollocked!

The local police along with the firemen were called. They were casually informed that there had been a spillage of petrol in the yard. The implication being that there may be a possibility of an explosion!

The firemen took a very different view and asked us to evacuate the exchange. Plus the police did likewise to most of the surrounding houses.

Meanwhile a bundle of requisitions were written and emergency calls made. Very soon an empty tanker was on its way to empty the generator fuel tank. Plus an additional supply tanker, this time with diesel, was coming to save the day.

Now, here lies the magic and power of the mighty requisition. They are made out in three copies, signed in numerous places but seldom checked. That was the GPO for you.

The police were pleased to have something to do rather than drink tea. The firemen were pleased to have a real emergency to practice on. We were pleased to join our external engineer colleagues down the local cafe. Then, once all had been completed; and households returned to normal, we simply carried on as if nothing had happened.

Arthur was ashen faced for days but we all agreed not to mention it to anyone. Future audits may have indicated an anomaly but nothing was ever questioned. In fact the only question was; where did the telephonists go when we evacuated the building?

The answer was simple enough; nowhere! We had forgotten to tell them. Thus, hidden up there on the third floor, they had worked throughout the whole hazardous event totally oblivious to any danger!

I did not have to wait long to experience yet another requisition balls up. One of the most useful items that came on my newly honed radar was Swarfega. This iconic green gel was used for cleaning oil or grease from your hands. This was accomplished without removal of the natural oils of the skin and really did work wonders. We used it all the time and most wash rooms continually smelled of the slightly scented aroma of the stuff.

That particular Monday, bored with looking out of the window, I had been de-constructing a Strowger switch and was covered with Oildag. This was a thick black oil. Searching in the wash room for a tin of Swarfega I noticed that we were down to our last tin. A quick check in the store room confirmed this impending disaster and off I went to tell Stan.

He was well pleased as this proved conclusively that his existence was valid; another requisition was under way.

Not wishing to mess about, Stan went for four dozen tins. This was probably enough for a couple of years. Unfortunately for Stan he ticked four dozen packets on the requisition and thus his fate was sealed.

The following week a large lorry appeared at the front gate and pooped his horn. Again Stan, bristling with importance, wandered down with his pen to sign off the delivery. The lorry was filled with four dozen boxes each marked Swarfega. Stan, flummoxed, and not wishing to look out of his comfort zone with the delivery crew, signed the proffered delivery note.

Watching this 'tableau' with interest we noted an opportunity and sprung into action. There followed a quickly formed chain of telephone engineers passing the boxes along the line into the yard. Each of their faces silently displaying the mental thoughts within,

'Where can I flog this stuff?', 'How many can I nick before anyone notices?', 'I wonder if one of these cases will fit in the back of the car?'

At the same time Stan was thinking, *'How the fuck am I going to get out of this one?'*

Stan, to his credit, took it stoically, his solution simple. The sooner this stuff had 'disappeared' the safer he would be. We packed tins in the store rooms. We packed them into cupboards. We packed them into toilets. We packed them into cars. And within two days they had evaporated.

The exchange had enough tins of Swarfega for 20 years. Each engineer had enough Swarfega for their extended families for decades. And, the rest of the Civil Service found it hard to requisition Swarfega for a year as central stores restocked. I personally never bought a tin again. Nor for that matter did any of my friends.

Actually there were a couple of things that were never purloined from the exchange. First was the strange white soap found in all the toilets. This was Civil Service soap and, as such, had the royal crest neatly imprinted on the side.

It didn't smell of anything, it didn't lather up and it didn't remove dirt. In fact it didn't do much at all. But, it did have 'royal' approval. What it really contained was a mystery, however, one thing's for sure, there was not much soap! And, as an item on the 'not-wanted' list, it was always in plentiful supply.

The other item was the bizarre toilet paper. This

was hard, tough and....shiny. Yes, shiny toilet paper! It did however, along with a proud *'Property of the GPO',* display some very useful information; *'Please now wash your hands'.* The guys often would comment on the suitability of wiping your arse on the property of the GPO. However, I am sure that some did not follow the rest of the instructions!

I did a double-take and laughed recently when I noticed one of these toilet rolls for sale on eBay. Believe it or not I was actually considering bidding; just for old time's sake. Unbelievably though, it shot up in price and eventually sold for about £10. Perhaps I should have nicked a few rolls after all!

The final proof of the strange power of the requisition came with the battle of the stores wall. In front of the stores stood a 20 metre long, 2 metre high crumbling white wall. The reason for its existence had long since been forgotten; and it was now a hindrance. Blocking the parking for the ever increasing fleet of green vans and restricting access to the rear of the building.

A year before my arrival, as part of a general tidy up, a requisition had been raised to have this wall re-painted. Now, a requisition had been activated to have it removed. However, as was usual with the GPO, nothing was ever that simple. One requisition was long overdue another was acted upon with undue haste. One bright sunny morning this left two different sets of contractors at odds in the yard!

You have to appreciate here that these contractors could not have their work signed off, and thus paid for, until completed. So we had one team determined to paint this wall, the other intent on demolishing it. Stan valiantly tried his best to referee this stand off, and finally reached a compromise. The painting could begin; he would judge it as complete and sign off the requisition for payment. Meanwhile demolition would start at the other end!

So, there we were, looking out of the windows at two teams working on the wall. The first furiously painting a nice white colour at one end; and the second rapidly removing bricks from the other end. Even to the seasoned GPO eyes of the guys at the Hill, this was a jaw dropping moment. Thankfully, this didn't last until the two teams met in the middle. Stan signed off the painting and they departed, leaving the demolition guys to finish the job.

John nicely summed up our thoughts as we sloped off to tea break,

"I don't fucking believe that!" he proclaimed with a shaking head.

CHAPTER 11-Dirty Jobs and a Wage Snatch

It is time now to introduce another resident character; Tiny. Now unlike Little John in the Robin Hood stories, this nickname was not ironic. He was bloody tiny. One of the cleaners at the Hill, his main speciality was the boiler room. Plus anything deemed sooty, mucky, dirty or smelly.

This was, in no way, forced upon him. He actually loved getting covered in gunge, and revelled in jobs that others shied away from. Standing at about 4 feet 5 inches he was also able to squeeze into corners inaccessible to his colleagues!

His small size did cause a major problem once though, in the toilets. Inside were a row of urinals, one of which was at child's height. Don't ask me why, this was the GPO! Tiny, obviously, used this one being the only one he could just reach with his equipment.

At that time the floor tiles were damaged and were being replaced by a tiler. He decided that to get a better match, he would remove the small 6 inch step up to the urinals, tile right up to the wall and replace the step afterwards. As he was simply removing tiles this particular day, he left a simple sign by the door urging caution.

Tiny was out in the yard and was busting for a piss. He rushed into the toilets at full speed only to be confronted by a missing step; and his urinal several inches too high. The only quick solution, which came to his mind, was to jump up and down and piss at the same time. This to the great amusement of the guys hiding in there having a fag.

He scored with 50%, the rest he dried off his trousers by the boiler!

As you would expect, his work style 'modus operandi' left him continually in a grimy state, and you could normally smell him coming. He would enter the canteen with his huge boots, rough trousers tied with string, a very tight waist coat and long sleeve shirt; all these being a dusty grey colour. What colour they actually started out as, I have no idea. The telephonists, in particular, took exception to this appearance and would move away as soon as he arrived. Tiny never noticed anything!

He was also less than welcome when the Blood Donation team arrived at Crouch End. As this event meant time off, everyone wanted to go. And several cars, vans and bikes would descend on the chosen site. As a new guy I was a bit wary of what was going to happen, the others all seemed macho about the whole thing. So I put aside any concerns of blood loss, needles and pain and joined them to do my bit.

We all sat in a row waiting our turn. There were fitters, installers, pole guys, hole guys in fact everyone; and Tiny. When I entered, I was shown to a canvas bed and very quickly was pumping my 'pint' into a plastic bag. This hung on the side of the bed. Next to me several nurses were wiping grime off of Tiny's arms with some alcohol solution 'tutting' as they went. It appeared that they always had to clean him down at every blood donation session.

Now, normally you remained for a few minutes to rest, have a cup of tea and a biscuit, then departed. But the large macho external guys scoffed at this and got up to immediately leave. Tiny, not wanting to be left behind went with them. As I finished my tea and made for the door I was met by two large macho external guys passed out on the floor. Little skinny Tiny was helping a nurse fan them!

Now, at the time I arrived at the Hill the guys, if they wished, could be paid in cash. To that end one of the external engineers would drive to Crouch End and return with a box full of named envelopes. Each of these envelopes would contain their weekly wage. The wages would then be distributed by the TOA.

On the appointed day it was not unusual for large numbers of engineers to congregate in the test room. Here they would longingly look out of the window waiting for the arrival of the cash. Each mentally spending the overtime element before handing the remaining envelope over to the wife! Then, on its arrival, they would casually disperse to the ground floor to be paid.

Of course the GPO took this delivery very seriously. In fact they took it so seriously that a 'guard' was appointed to assist the driver. A guard was needed who would scare any potential robbers. A guard was required who could do battle with villains and save the day.

Bernie, on the other hand, had a slightly different view,

'Who the fuck don't we need for 3 hours?'

So Tiny, all 4 feet 5 inches of him, was the chosen one!

It was a warm spring Friday, and the world was looking good from the windows of the test room. Blossom was in the trees outside and the banter was swaying back and forth within. Some of the guys were a bit miffed as the delivery was a bit late and there was a danger of this event eating into their coffee break.

Suddenly, in the road appearing from the left there emerged the van. Tiny was sat in the passenger seat with the money box on his lap. With equal suddenness a large black car raced forward from the right, crashing into the van head on. Luckily, at this stage, the van had nearly stopped outside the door, and the car had only travelled a few metres from its parking place. Thus the resulting crash merely stalled both vehicles.

The next few minutes appeared as a sequence from a film. Three large guys, with stockings pulled over their faces, exploded from the car. They each brandished a menacing cosh and were clearly meaning business. Tiny immediately swung into action. His door was flung open, the box thrown up into the air and he ran like an Olympic sprinter away from the scene.

The robbers quickly scooped up handfuls of scattered envelops, retreated to the car and reversed at speed back up the road.

Inside the test room nobody breathed, nobody spoke and nobody moved. The background chatter of Strowger was finally broken by an insightful and educated comment,

"Oh well! There goes my fucking coffee break. I'm going to have to hang around for hours now!"

"Fuck me, Tiny didn't put up much of a fight did he?" followed another's caring observation.

With this, they mostly evaporated away like a cinema crowd at the end of the show. Hot sweet tea was administered to the van driver, police were called and Stan was on the phone to Crouch End.

Unfortunately for Bernie someone was also on the phone to the local press. And, almost at the same time as the police, a reporter arrived.

This normally would not be an issue except that Tiny chose this moment to peer round the corner and amble back. Overhearing Tiny explain that he was the guard, the reporter descended on him like a hawk on a sparrow. Photos were taken of Tiny stood by the van. Photos were taken of Tiny at the main door. And cleverly, a photo was taken of him stood next to one of the policemen. This, of course, greatly exaggerated his diminutive size and the story was writing itself.

The following day; Saturday, the local paper hit the streets. Front page headlines declared,

'Midget hero stands up to robbers!'

Under this slightly misleading headline came a photo of Tiny next to a policeman. Dressed in his normal attire he was not a great advert for GPO dress code or their ability to match appropriate folk to a job.

Thankfully no mention was made of the 30 or so fit and healthy engineers who casually had watched this drama unfold.

Bernie was dragged over the coals for this and returned from a meeting at Crouch End white faced and glum. His parting comment on disappearing into the fog of his office was,

"Arabs! I bet it was Arabs!"

CHAPTER 12-Butt Resistance and Listening In

A faded, yellowing ancient sign hung gathering dust behind the switchboards. Under the bold heading of **'Secrecy as to Telephone Messages'** it stated,

'Telephone messages that come into your knowledge by any means are to be regarded as strictly confidential.'

This being part of the Post Office Protection Act 1884, apparently.

That was all well and good, but it didn't say that you couldn't listen in did it? In fact 'listening in' was regarded by most engineers as a perk of the job. It was undertaken at any time of the day and filled in for the time between tea breaks. This, of course, when simply looking out of the window had become a chore.

By listening in to subscriber conversations the guys quickly became aware of the more 'interesting' numbers to follow. They would also target telephone kiosks, as these calls could be interrupted or cross connected to make the entertainment more fun.

This listening in ability was aided and abetted by the most useful tool in the telephone engineer's armoury. The Buttinski or Butt!

The real identity for this piece of kit was GPO Telephone No. 280. The name Buttinski came from a Polish guy centuries ago. He was famous for forcing his advice on important people. One day he gave the wrong advice to the wrong person and was duly executed. Since then a Buttinski has become a sarcastic label for someone who enters a conversation without permission!

So, it was a perfect name for the perfect tool. The Butt was basically a rubberised handset. It had a dial, and was fitted with a multi-use plug, with which, you could plug it in to almost anywhere in the telephone exchange. You could listen in without detection or speak by pressing a small red button on its side.

A typical 'educational' use for this instrument was listening in to the calls coming and going from the local brothel. Here you could listen to the requirements of potential customers, listen to arguments between the girls and their pimps and wonder at the gymnastics as the girls shared experiences from one brothel to the next.

If you were lucky a phone would be left off the hook by the bedside; so as not to disturb the girls during 'business'. The guys would be roaring with laughter as the grunts, puffs and groans filtered through the line. This, naturally, as a young guy was highly enlightening. However having experienced the paraffin round for several years I was learning nothing new.

One of the more unfortunate down sides to the Butt was its introduction of a small amount of resistance on the line. This resistance could slightly degrade the call. Now a small bit of resistance is okay but when 8 engineers are all sat there listening, each with his own Butt, each adding resistance. Well, I think you get the picture. In fact I strongly believe that the girls at the brothel did as well.

One afternoon, sometime in-between the after lunch smoke break and afternoon tea break, a shout went up from the second floor. An argument over a client between two prostitutes had been picked up. This was not to be missed, so up we rushed Butts at the ready.

At first only a few of us were listening, but the call was getting quieter. As a few more joined, the call degraded further and the girls had to shout. By the time that Butt number 8 was plugged in it was almost impossible to hear; and one of the girls shouted,

"If that's you fucking engineers doing that, I going to kill ya!"

Eight Butts were removed like a synchronised swimming manoeuvre, and with a laugh the fun was over. I still have my Butt. It hangs gathering dust in the garage, and each time I walk by I think of the stories it could tell! (It actually features on the front cover of this book!)

This type of pastime was not unusual and, when times got quiet, was orchestrated. Telephone kiosks were a popular target; especially as we had one within sight of the Hill. The best way to get the fun going was to cross connect two kiosks allowing 4 people to suddenly find themselves on the call! This would quickly progress to an argument as each of the 4 declared priority. They would then demand that the others leave the call.

It was not unusual for the 4 protagonists to

continue talking over each other, each refusing to clear down. This, of course, was highly entertaining for us but bloody infuriating for them. Just to get things more complex the Buttinski also joined in. Suddenly there were 6 or 7 people all demanding priority. Our pretended priority, naturally, was declared the greatest!

It must be hard to understand the tolerance of those people in these modern technological times. However, this was an age when disconnections and line noise were normal. Dialling out to a 'no tone' was expected. And some folk even had to share one telephone line between two houses, the infamous 'party' line.

On another occasion I was sitting with the guys on the test desk. On this occasion we were testing lines and dial speeds for the engineers out on the patch. Here we had the luxury of switchboard headsets thus multi listening was not an issue.

Now, before actually testing a faulty line it was routinely listened to for a genuine reason. We did not want to screw up someone's conversation, by testing, while they were on the line. What thoughtful chaps.

Bill, the TO on the desk, was waiting to test a line. It had been reported that morning as 'noisy'. However, each time he listened a call was in progress. So, he hung on in there waiting for them to end the call. A smile appeared on his face and he asked us to join him listen in.

The call was between an elderly sounding guy and his mistress. He was, to put it bluntly, shagging her over the phone. Grunts coming from his end; sighs and moans from hers. Each, I presume, had a phone in one hand and was performing masturbation with the other. To make this more interesting he kept pausing and whispering as someone, probably his wife, passed by his room!

Now this was becoming a bit boring and Bill was losing patience, so, as the guy announced that he thought he was coming, Bill interrupted,

"Really! Well I wish you would hurry up," he said, "I'm waiting to test the fucking line!"

Bill then began the silent countdown with his fingers. On the count of 9 the ENG light glowed red. He answered and explained politely that this 'cross connection' was probably caused by an exchange fault or a crossed line. No sir, it was impossible for engineers to listen to people's calls. Yes sir, we will be looking into this as a matter of urgency. Thanks bye.

"Well, that's one way to clear the line!" he chuckled.

Karma did bite back at Bill sometime later in a 'timing is everything' moment. He was infatuated with one of the telephonists and would always hang around on the ground floor for her arrival. The process was always the same. She would arrive on her bike, park it against the wall by the lift and disappear upwards. Meanwhile Bill would casually stand around pretending to look busy while desperately thinking of something witty to say.

Naturally we didn't help this process by taking the piss at every opportunity and suggesting very inappropriate topics for him to raise by way of conversation.

This all came to a head one morning with several of us in attendance. She arrived but was obviously busting for a pee as she parked her bike and rushed into the men's toilets on the ground floor. This was an action clearly indicating some urgency!

Out of the quiet room came Bill. He was somewhat flustered to see the bike already there and ourselves casually watching events unfold. So in a moment of bravado, and clearly thinking that the object of his desires had ascended in the lift, he rushed over to the bike.

He lifted the bike saddle to his nose and leaning back took a deep, prolonged sniff. He thought that this would cause a laugh and take the heat off of our mickey taking. Unfortunately, at the very moment that the bike was at its highest point and the sniff at its loudest; she reappeared out of the toilet.

The horrified look on her face was only beaten by the look of shear shock and horror on Bill's. Without saying a word she entered the lift, pressed for up and slowly ascended. It was an open lift system and her eyes never left Bill's all the way up until she thankfully passed from view. Bill stood rigid with the saddle parked under his nose during this whole process. We stood motionless wishing we were somewhere else!

Finally breathing out he casually parked the bike against the wall, said "fuck it" and walked up the stairs a beaten man. We all looked at each other, burst out laughing and ran off to share this event with everyone else. Poor Bill was mortified for weeks but fate does sometimes play unusual tricks.

Several years later he married the same telephonist. It was his personal apology for the embarrassment caused that had started them talking; they didn't stop talking apparently and that was that!

There are probably grandchildren walking about today that owe their existence to a bike saddle!

CHAPTER 13-Idle Pastimes and Sex Shows

Lunchtime at the Hill was a time to relax. After all, work was tough, work was hard, and we needed some wind down time. Normally you could suggest perhaps a game of cards, but by lunchtime we had had enough of cards. Maybe service the car, well no, that would have been done during the illegal coffee break. So when there was no sun for a tan, we had snooker, table tennis and other pursuits.

These were, as usual, undertaken in a very competitive fashion. The full size snooker table had the air and tension of a professional competition, as pairs battled against each other. At the other end of the games room, sweaty bodies gasped for breath as the table tennis ball was pounded from one end of the table to the other.

After years of this regime some of these guys were very good at one, or both, of these activities. This, of course, helped the newcomers to improve. The end result being a large number of highly trained, capable snooker and table tennis players! It is understandable why these guys had no energy left for actual work in the afternoon.

As an alternative there was, obviously, the pub; but this seemed to be left mainly for special events like leaving do's, marriages and funerals. Apart from Wally, that is.

Wally spent all his life in the pub. He had bottles of rum in his locker, in his car and in his tool box. An ex sailor he was perpetually drunk, and you could smell him and the rum from 20 paces. You would find him, some days, leaning against an equipment rack fast asleep. Other days he would be snoring rum soaked fumes in the locker room where he had sat on arrival, and not moved since.

He had a real problem but no one seemed to do anything about it. Today there would be counselling. In those days, there was just the slippery slope to an early grave. And that's what caught up with Wally. It was the only time that we did not go to the pub to toast a passing colleague. It just did not seem appropriate!

The pub did, however, provide one source of entertainment; strippers and sex shows. One of the nearby Hackney pubs had a reputation for occasional strip tease shows. This, in itself, was not such a great draw, but this place had a unique selling point. Sometimes a live sex show followed the strippers. The landlord had hit on a winner, and when word was put out, he was sure of a full house. The crowds were there for the beer, but also to see blow jobs and live sex shows on the stage!

One Friday, word had reached us of a possible show for that lunchtime. A few of the guys were going and I, for purely educational purposes, decided to join them on the trip. We arrived a bit late as John had insisted on eating chips before we got there. And as we walked into the bar, a naked stripper was already giving someone a rather vigorous blow-job.

The 'recipient' was stood there, knees knocking, with his trousers around his ankles. His face betrayed a look halfway between bliss and fear. Her 'performance' over, the stripper was leaving for the toilets when our chauffeur, John, walked through the door. As she passed him she planted a huge 'tongue swallowing' kiss on his lips. As we bought the beers he walked on towards us with a big grin on his face.

Our combined aghast expressions were cut short as another stripper entered the bar and started her routine. It was all the normal stuff, but when finally naked, she then proceeded to search the audience for a willing volunteer. She didn't have to search for long. One guy, strongly egged on by his mates, stepped up to the mark and entered the performance. He soon had joined her on the floor for the finale of the whole show.

Naturally some of the audience pushed forward for a better view, unfortunately too far forward. And, very quickly, a fight erupted. Now here you had a good mix of brick layers, plasterers and lorry drivers; not the shrinking violet types. Oh! And a few telephone engineers. Therefore, the ensuing fight quickly got out of hand.

Chairs, bottles, glasses and various bodies were flying through the air. Tables were overturned and beer was everywhere. Now, at this stage, I would have liked to tell you of my rush to join the melee, fists flying. However remembering that I was there just for educational purposes, I stuck to the wall like wallpaper and casually sipped my Double Diamond.

It was then that I noticed him. Still there on the floor amid the spilt beer, overturned tables and stomping feet. He was oblivious to the breaking glasses and shouts. The volunteer, he was still pumping away on top of the naked stripper. He had started so he was going to finish!

At this stage the landlord was ringing the bar bell and shouting "Police!" and "Get Out!" This had the magical effect of dispersing the audience like snow on hot coals. We quickly left, nervously swapping notes on this unforgettable experience. Luckily with just a few bruises and scrapes between us.

Driving back in John's car it seemed like a good moment to mention his lingering kiss with the stripper. As you might expect, the fact that she had just had someone else's knob in her mouth didn't go down too well. He spent the rest of the afternoon gurgling with white royalty approved soap!

One other summer favourite was the swimming baths near Clissold Park. This was urged on by Ernie, another TTA, who had amazingly smelly feet. He reasoned that hours in the chlorine infused pool would help. It didn't.

As an aside, a few years later when 'Odour Eaters' shoe insoles hit the market, he tried them out to solve his problem. All that happened was a continuation of his smelly feet, plus 'Odour Eaters' that also stank! Disgruntled he put them in an envelope and sent them back to the manufacturer asking for a refund. He never got a reply!

As for Clissold swimming pool, as usual with these guys, they were not content just to swim. There had to be an element of competition or, at least, something to boast about back at the Hill. It was rather unfortunate, therefore, that one lunchtime we arrived as a group were training for Personal Survival and Life Saving awards. It was even more unfortunate that, when asked what was happening, we were told about the difficulties.

Apparently there were four levels of Personal Survival; bronze, silver, gold and honours. Following these, there were bronze badge and finally bronze cross Life Saving awards.

"Very difficult," explained the instructor, "It could take you years," he helpfully added.

"Bollocks!" said Ernie, "bet we could do it in a couple of months!"

With this *'red rag to a bull'* challenge well noted, the swimming baths became a regular target at lunchtime. We spent months working through those awards almost killing ourselves in the process. More and more pull-ups were practised on the racks, life saving and first aid theory was swotted and various swimming garments appeared drying all over the exchange.

Many months later all the awards had been won, the gloss went off swimming and we never returned to Clissold swimming pool. It was back to snooker again!

For me, some of it did prove useful. On a later holiday to Cornwall, as I sat on the beach watching the rough wave's crash against the rocks, a girl dropped off the rocks into the water. Hey! I had been trained for this, so in I rushed. The sea was rough, very rough and the undercurrents were pulling hard. The training had shown how to calm a frightened, drowning person. What it did not prepare you for was wrestling with a drowning person having an epileptic fit! No! The instructor had forgotten to mention that one.

It was a bit like trying to calm an octopus. Her legs and arms were going everywhere and I was struggling. Luckily, just as my feet hit the sand, a surf-boarder pulled up alongside. We pulled her half on the board and rushed her onto the beach where a previously dozing lifeguard took over. She was coming round and speaking to us, she seemed fine, so I quickly slipped away.

A couple of days later; as I parked my dad's old battered Vauxhall Viva down by the beach, I was pointed at. A young girl was standing next to a large, menacing looking bloke and was pointing in my direction. No, actually she was pointing at me! This didn't look good. My mind went into overdrive thinking what I had done wrong, but I was with my girlfriend, I couldn't have done anything wrong! With that, the large gentleman rushed over to the car.

I quickly changed into reverse gear but had forgotten that the engine was now switched off! There was nothing for it; I wound down the window trying to look innocent,

"I want to thank you for saving my daughter," he said, shaking me by the hand.

"Er! That's okay," I said, somewhat relieved.

With that he walked off, and I sat letting my heart drop to a normal rate. I am not sure if 'saving' was correct; but at least one of those lunchtime 'idle pastimes' finally paid dividends!

CHAPTER 14-Bad Timing and Washer Japes

Arthur was back in the TOA chair and he was determined not to repeat the oil tank fiasco. With that experience firmly fixed in his mind everything was double checked, twice. He was becoming a pain with the signing-on book and extremely boring with signing off.

The signing-on book was located on the ground floor and, as the name suggests, was signed by everyone on arrival. At 8.00 am a red line was drawn and all signatures after that were answerable to Bernie. This would mean sitting for ages in his fog filled room listening to him bleat on about Arabs always being late in the desert!

Normally Stan allowed a 5 to 10 minute grace before drawing the red line. Arthur was on the dot! Signing off was a different matter. People generally congregated in the test room about 4.45 pm expecting to leave. Stan would give the nod about 4.50ish, and you would not want to be coming up the stairs at that moment. However, Arthur was watching the second hand on the master clock and the nod was not coming until the last second struck home. Not good.

The master clock was an interesting piece of kit. It fed electrical signals throughout the exchange. These signals ran all the clocks and, more importantly, all the equipment that determined telephone call costs. The master clock ruled. It could never be incorrect. It was a God. Well, to Arthur anyway.

It seemed to me that there was a simple solution to our problem. It was just a matter of time! In the afternoon, during one of Arthur's many trips to the loo (just count the tea breaks!), we attacked. The master clock could be stepped on with a relay. This movement was reflected throughout the exchange, but there was no clock in the loo. When Arthur came back, time had moved on 30 minutes!

The first glance at the clock produced a double take from Arthur; time was flying this afternoon. However, he checked his watch and we thought we were done. Much to our surprise with a,

"Fucking rubbish, I knew it; fucking Japanese!"

He synchronized his newly acquired, knocked off, Seiko to the 'master' and settled back, grumbling, in his chair.

There seemed to be a lot of suspicious Seiko watches doing the rounds that year. I now think they were genuine, and Seiko were flooding the market with their old models before the introduction of the first ever quartz models a year later! Arthur was persuaded to buy his because 'Seiko' meant *'exquisite'* in Japanese!

So, it was 4.45 pm according to the master clock and we were filling out the test room. Arthur's desk was at the end by the door and he was watching the master clock intently. I don't know why, but he had a change of heart and gave us the nod at 4.55 pm. Except for Arthur, and a couple of guys guarding the test desk, we were quickly all gone.

The first moment he began to question time, space and everything was a call from a neighbouring telephone exchange.

"Nobody is answering the special faults phone," he complained.

"Of course they're not; they have all gone," Arthur replied.

"Why have they all gone?" asked the caller, becoming confused.

"Because HERE we do things by the book!" Arthur rallied with a raised voice.

The phone went down and the guys on the test desk slunk down in their chairs. A few minutes later a similar call arrived and, after checking his Seiko then glancing up at the clock, a similar response was given. The guys slunk down further; this was not going to end well.

The final straw was a grumpy call from the switchboard room. The head supervisor had now been waiting ages for the engineers to finish adjusting the clocks. She had seen the clocks move, and had been phoning down for updates. Nobody seemed to be answering and she was losing patience.

"When are your people going to put the clocks back?" she opened.

"What do you mean?" a worried Arthur responded.

"I've checked TIM (the GPO speaking clock, see end of chapter) and we are 30 minutes fast!" she tersely explained.

"Er! Any minute now," an enlightened Arthur

mumbled.

The phone went down and he looked up for a chat with the test desk guys. They seemed to have miraculously disappeared. A quick call to TIM confirmed the worst; his beloved master clock was wrong. Adjustments were made and the whole exchange clicked back to real time. Coincidently, it was now exactly 5.00 pm.

The next day, expecting a bollocking, we were surprised by the calm. However, it would appear that we were all marked as late. Arthur had arrived early, moved the hands on the signing-on room clock forward 30 minutes, and drawn the red line! Touché!

Seiko watches were not the only items often appearing for sale at the Hill. There was always something. It could be shirts, shoes, radios or even wall paper. Anything you needed turned up sooner or later. Two of the most frequent were large slabs of Cheddar cheese, and chocolate Brazil nuts! Where all this stuff came from I will never know, and naturally nobody ever asked!

That afternoon though all was forgotten as a new diversion had arrived. Four new Ford Escort vans had been delivered and we were all over them. They were not for us, obviously, these were for the installers; and after the old Morris vans they were quite an excitement.

It did not take long to discover the amazingly powerful windscreen washers and took even less to put them to good use. A quick twist with a pin and the powerful stream of water shot at right angles from the van.

I remember watching from the window and laughing as these guys expertly manoeuvred in the yard. The washers were being used as water pistols, with the objective being, to squirt the windscreen of your rival. Naturally a few bumps and scrapes occurred along the way. At this rate these vans wouldn't last very long.

Unfortunately the guys took this to the next level when they realised there were other targets. If you kept your finger on the button long enough, a whole bus queue could be soaked as you drove by. Plus you could single out individuals like old people with a stick or ladies with a pram for example. These hits could be tallied and scores shared. Fun was being had.

Of course, it did not take long for the complaints to arrive. The miscreants found themselves swapped back into old Morris vans and the streets were safe again. Just in the nick of time actually. They had planned to fill the water tanks with ink the following week!

(Dialling TIM gave access to the GPO speaking clock. However, only the management of the GPO could not see the irony in having a female voice record the announcements for a site with a male name! BT finally saw the joke and updated to a male voice in 1985, his name was Brian!)

CHAPTER 15-Suntans, Meters and FNF

Every so often a problem would arise in the switchboard room and Stan would send up a willing volunteer to address the issue. He felt it was time for me to gain experience of this mystical third floor and up I was sent with Sid. Now let's be clear, this was not an area where you could overtly mess about. It was run by an elderly head supervisor who ruled with an iron fist.

She was as strict as Captain Bligh and twice as nasty. Bernie, in particular, was petrified of her and never ventured past the second floor. The other telephonists, therefore, were always pleased by some diversion and we were it.

They would sit in front of the switchboard and often complain of frayed faulty line cords. This necessitated us removing the back and lower front of the switchboard to gain access to the offending item. While we were busy at the back, they were busy in the front; crossing and uncrossing legs, pulling up stockings and generally trying their best to make this very difficult for us. The occasional,

"You two nearly done back there?" was met by a stifled laugh from us.

However, we didn't know it at the time but we were as much entertainment for them as we would have liked them to be for us!

The proof of this was the scores found chalked on the upper roof one day. This was where the telephonists could take a smoke break or get some fresh air. This was the highest point of the exchange and overlooked everything.

The second floor also had a roof. This was flat and perfect for a summer ritual that all the young guys loved; sunbathing. We would spend hours up there in the sun and the competition for best tan was fierce. Ben was excluded from this, obviously, as he had a head start. We would rush up there as soon as lunch arrived and leave it to the last second before descending again. There would then be a session of comparing arms to see who was winning.

As you would expect, this led to experimentation with various oils to help this process along. And I am not talking shop bought oils here. These were the home made variety. The most popular seemed to be a mixture of cold cream and olive oil; these two ingredients being joined in differing quantities.

I tried this mixture on a holiday with my girlfriend years later. We fried, and spent several days shut in a caravan unable to move!

Now while sunbathing on the roof we were, naturally, in various stages of undress. After all, no one could see could they? Well actually they could. From their vantage point on the third floor, the girls were keeping score. Points were being given for body, tan, muscles and bulge!

Only a routine inspection of the lightening rods at the top of the exchange exposed this competition. There on the wall, which looked over the second floor, were our marks. Thankfully it would appear that we all had nicknames, and we never managed to work out who was winning. We did manage to work out one though; Ben, by the size of the bulge!

Like the switchboard duties another job appeared from time to time; but this one was unwelcome. As the new boy, I was handed this boring routine on several occasions, and hated it. However it did have perks.

The routine in question was testing meters. Every subscriber in the exchange had their own unique meter. This recorded calls and was used to determine your bill. These meters had to be tested and there were 20 thousand of them.

This boring task required the engineer to connect to each meter in turn, and use a special device to pump calls through them. A hundred was enough to check all was working okay. After which the amount of 'test call' numbers were carefully logged so that the subscriber would not pay for them.

Naturally this could be beneficial for locally based family and friends. Their meters could have 10 test calls made but 100 logged. Conversely, people you really didn't like could have 200 test calls made with only 100 logged! Even better, if a local shop or business really pissed someone off they could get several hundred test calls on their meter with just 100 logged. The possibilities for 'adjustments' were endless but purely theoretical!

The other odd occurrence was the small number of disconnected meters that were miraculously reconnected just after meter testing was announced, and just before it began. This strange coincidence just goes to demonstrate how sharp these guys were. They could find and locate faults before anyone had tested anything!

After my unwelcome meter testing experience Stan would often put me on to Special Faults with Fred to bring my brain back from the dead. This Special Faults line was one of several positions at the Hill where you passed faults out to other exchanges and, in return, received others back. It could be busy but always interesting. Fault dockets had to be completed, the A566. Plus a whole new world of mnemonics and three letter abbreviations had to be memorised.

My favourites and most well used were FNF, meaning fault not found, and RWT, meaning right when tested. These two 'get out of jail' abbreviations were heaven sent as they allowed completion of an otherwise baffling fault. This would often then re-appear for someone else later!

Another fault expression has been used by me ever since those days; *'One leg diss'.* An expression that highlights one wire disconnected on a pair of subscriber wires. This would obviously make the pair useless. However this was habitually used by telephone engineers to denote a person who was somewhat lacking in the brain department! Thus, nodding in someone's direction and uttering,

"O-L-D!" or "One leg!" enabled us to be defamatory without the individual in question understanding the implication.

This position also gave one of the more exciting opportunities in a telephone exchange, the emergency 999 call trace. This would normally be a call trace demanded from the switchboard, and could be a real emergency. Fred and I would rush like maniacs from one switch to the next, Butt in hand, up and down ladders, back-tracking the call to its origin. Finally, breathlessly we would give the originating number to the telephonist.

There was always an element of competition between myself and Fred as to who could do this the fastest. And, for once at the Hill, this probably led to saving lives. However I did suspect that the telephonists sometimes called these call traces down, when they were bored, just to see who was quickest!

There was another interesting by-product of sitting next to a Special Faults phone all day. That was the fact that sitting and talking on this phone was probably legitimate. Therefore no one took much notice if you appeared to be doing an awful lot of it.

The first week I was there Fred spent hours each day chatting up a local office receptionist. He had first spoke to her on the test desk when tracing a fault. Now he was taking this opportunity to get to know her better. And these conversations were certainly getting hotter by the day.

He had never seen the lady in question but she certainly sounded nice, and Fred wanted to take this to the next level. So in a true, brave, and manly fashion, he sent an external engineer to check her out. The engineer in question was more than happy to comply and soon returned to report back his findings,

"Blonde hair," he opened with.

"Great," enthused Fred.

"High heels," added our secret agent.

"Better still," said Fred.

"About 30," the engineer continued.

"That's good," responded Fred now getting even keener.

"No mate, I mean about 30 stone!" added the engineer, with a wink in my direction.

"Fuck it!" exclaimed Fred, "that's two bloody weeks wasted there!"

What a gentleman!

CHAPTER 16-Cable Chamber Secrets and Porn

One of the nice things about being accepted as one of the lads, was the ability to explore the Hill unsupervised. Here was a huge building full of strange equipment, unexplained rooms and mysterious noises.

Here was stuff that, with the wrong touch, could take off-air 20,000 subscribers or blow you up, depending on where you stuck your fingers! And I loved to explore; or was I just nosey?

It was with great interest then that I took these opportunities to roam the Hill and educate myself. One of the eeriest and mystifying parts was the cable chamber. It was deadly quiet and spooky. Here was a huge, long, dark underground chamber containing the massive telephone cables and trunk cables from other exchanges. It also contained some mystery rooms.

Luckily, by now, I had found the location of the exchange spare key box while snooping in the storeroom. Thus well armed, I went to investigate.

There were three of these mystery rooms all locked, and clearly unused for some considerable time. This was evident by the surrounding dust. On opening the first, I was disappointed to find.... nothing. Once there had been something here, some equipment perhaps or office furniture. This was evident by the large screw holes left in both the walls and the floor. However I lost interest and moved on.

The second door was to expose something far more exciting. And I was to experience a double-take on entering. As the door creaked open I was met by dark shadows and a smell of dusty decay. On finding the light switch however, the resulting illumination exposed an intact deserted war room. The lighting was archaic; yellowed bulbs struggled to make any viewing easy. I would think you would have got more wattage from a cheap torch!

However, here it all was. Two fully equipped switchboards sat side by side, these complete with ancient chairs. Telephonist headsets, large and unlike any I had seen before, sat ready on each position. There were a few old black Bakelite phones plus some old dialling code books to one side.

On the wall, two candlestick wall phones in mint

condition hung gathering dust. On top of the switchboards sat two helmets proudly marked GPO. The walls were lined with old metal fire buckets each with a GR royal crest. Strangely these were still filled with sand.

I do not think this door had been opened for many years, it was a time warp. Later enquiries revealed the background. Luckily Frank, one of the more ancient TOs, was a font of historic knowledge. He had served at the Hill, off and on, for 30 years; almost from its beginning. Thus he was well aware of the room, its contents and history.

The only surprise for him was that it was still there. He had not ventured down to the cable chamber for years.

He explained that certain lines in the exchange were a priority; for example fire, police, military, government and ambulance etc. In an emergency these lines took priority over everyone else and, if need be, all else was cut off to save these few.

The switchboards hidden down in the cable chamber were installed at the outbreak of world war two, and would have been manned in any disaster. The object was to keep the aforementioned emergency lines running; even if bombing necessitated clearance of the exchange. Two telephonists would have managed the priorities and connected emergency calls from one place to another.

Now, the cable chamber was deep underground. A perfect bomb shelter you may say. However I wonder if any real thought had been given to the telephonists? How would they have actually got out of that cable chamber if the exchange was bombed? There was only one way in, that gone, you were stuck!

The empty room I had first found had once housed some metal beds, chairs, tables and even a water supply. These were now all long gone.

Anyway, here the remnants of a world war remained; patiently waiting!

The other door revealed more intrigue; recording equipment. Apparently the GPO had its own special team that aided both the police and security services in listening to and recording conversations. I assume, naturally, that this was all legal. I recognised a pair of old reel-to-reel tape recorders plus other unknown gizmos.

Apparently, these bits of kit would always receive and monitor calls from another exchange. Nothing originating from the Hill would be recorded here. These would have left the Hill on a special 'private wire' and would have been recorded at an exchange elsewhere. That's the way it worked. On this occasion I genuinely felt uneasy about standing in this place. I quickly locked up and left.

Most of the engineers seemed to be aware of these rooms, but held no interest.

"You will find these places in most exchanges."

Was the normal response whenever I raised the subject. However, John seemed to become far more interested when I mentioned the two candlestick wall phones.

"Really?" he said, "and in good nick?"

He went on to explain that these must be very important connections to national security. It would be a disaster for us all if they failed. Gosh! We ought to get down there quick and ensure that they still work okay. It's our duty, isn't it, to maintain this place to the best of our ability. In fact, it would be a far more responsible thing to do if we were to update these phones!

Therefore a packet of roll-up tobacco was exchanged for two new plastic wall phones. This resulted in one happy external engineer and a happier John. The next day the dormant war room housed two new, sparkling wall phones to blend in nicely with the other dusty historic items. The old, rather valuable, candlestick wall phones were recycled by John.

It's nice to know that at least one engineer had the nation's interest at heart!

As to the 'special recording' room; some years later one of the TOs uncovered some amplifiers on a group of those special private wires. They were hidden underneath some wooden hatches by the MDF; and were amplifying private wires passing through the Hill. No record of these wires existed anywhere, and no indication as to why they were there had been recorded. They could only be one thing.

Being bored at the time he decided to make some 'adjustments' on them just to see what would happen. The adjustments took the form of twisting every knob he could find and replacing the hatches.

The next day a very irate and flustered 'mystery' engineer arrived. He spent hours calibrating them all again; during which he made dozens of angry phone calls to an exchange further down the line. He did not accuse anyone with meddling, but the looks he gave said it all. Mess with this stuff again and you're fucked!

The other multi-tasking use for this dark cable chamber was occasional film shows. Now, I'm not talking Hollywood here, nor or am I talking Disney. This was also the porn show room. Every couple of months or so, a new supply of porn films would suddenly materialise. Where they came from is anyone's guess. However, the finger often pointed at the local nick!

Word quickly got about (we were a telecommunication team after all!) and a rapid whip round paid the rental for the films. A projector appeared from somewhere, was set up and a date set. This would normally be a lunch time, and it's surprising how many guys you could cram into this place and still breathe.

It was also surprising, to me, how many of the

guys would turn up with their lunch and munch away during the show. Looking back now, it's also astounding that some wag wasn't selling ice creams.

Normally there would be about three films, each of about 10 minutes long. This was long enough to raise the temperature alarmingly in the cable chamber. It's probably why only the younger guys attended. After all 30 plus guys, no air, lots of heat and excitement. That would have probably killed off some of the older ones!

The films themselves were grainy copies, badly made, well used and had an unfortunate ability to break just at an interesting moment. This would raise jeers, boo's and general shouting as our valiant projectionist struggled to reconnect. It was not unusual for various particles of food to be thrown if this happened more than once. This was a sight most Elizabethan stage actors would immediately recognise.

Nonetheless, it was not the films themselves that made this an event not to be missed; however educational the material. It was the banter. Endless comments ranged from,

"Looks like your wife Jim!" To "Wouldn't touch that with yours!" And "Always wondered what auntie Doris did!"

After the show much laughter could be heard as the crowd dispersed. And, some of the younger in the audience made notes for future reference!

I am not sure what would have happened if the GPO special branch or the police needed access to their recording room during a film show. Perhaps they would have simply joined the audience. Perhaps they were in the audience!

Also, what if the government had needed the war room for a national emergency? Would the guys have stopped the show? I doubt it!

CHAPTER 17-Batteries, Drugs and Funerals

The battery and power room was an interesting place. A massive room filled with long lines of huge black batteries. These were supplying direct current to the exchange in times of need. The strong acidic smell hit you when entering. It was very warm at all times. It was very light and seldom entered. So, let's think then, what could you usefully use this room for?

Well it did not take long for some enterprising engineers to find the answer; cannabis! (Well! It was the 60s) Cannabis plants seemed to love it in the battery room and came along nicely. I cannot vouch for the quality of leaf though, as they never grew sufficiently to crop. There was always a problem with a visit by some outsider or a battery alarm necessitating maintenance.

It was always fun to watch the owners of these plants rush downstairs if a battery alarm rang. They were not worried about battery loss or disappearing electrical current. The rush was to shift the plants before anyone else arrived. The plants themselves did not enjoy this shock and invariably died! These horticultural experiments went on for years before they finally gave up.

Once or twice someone would bring some real stuff in to share round. You would think that the old guys would shun this type of activity, but no. They always joined in and shoved some in the next roll-up.

If they were on the test desk, when this chemical experiment was under way, the subscribers suffered. I assume that those with faulty lines found it hard to understand why the engineer seemed to be giggling as the fault was explained and dealt with!

Smoking anything, in fact, was an art form at the Hill. Pipes, roll-ups, tailor made, cheroots, cigars even snuff. It all came and went as the guys sought the best 'hit'. Everyone always came back to roll-ups though. They were the cheapest option. Sid was a master of the thin roll-up. His finished product looked as though it contained only about two strands of tobacco.

When smoked, in the canteen, the lit end would zip along like a burning fuse and he was forever burning his lip on the last 'drag'. Others could be seen nursing the final puffs of a roll-up until the butt end was too small to hold. There seemed to be an unwritten contest amongst the older guys as to who could smoke the most from one cigarette!

One of the sad realities of working in a place with some ageing colleagues was the retirements. Now, it was not the retirements themselves that were sad. It was the inevitable consequences.

First came the announcement, and then came the gift whip-round. Next we enjoyed the tea with pink cake for all the exchange plus the retiree's wife. Then we had the embarrassing speeches. Then we had the EE with his knob-head speech where he got the guy's name wrong. Then we endured the retiree's response where he told everyone how he would miss them all. Then we waved him goodbye, then he was dead! Then we had the funeral.

Hard to understand at the time but it did seem to happen continually. Normal life span for the retiring engineers seemed to be about six months. My theory was that they were continually bored at the Hill with nothing really to do. Then actual life outside, with real daily interesting activities, was too much. They had been brain dead for years and it took a few months of real life to realise it!

CHAPTER 18-Fuses, Megger and Pistol Fun

An exchange was full of places, surfaces and equipment that could give quite a whack of voltage if you touched it at the wrong time. This was a constant danger as you worked throughout the Hill and I got caught out many times. Often you would hear,

"Buzz..wow!..fuck it!"

And then the continued whistling of the victim as he progressed with his work as though nothing had happened. This was an occupational hazard. However, it was not always minor and not always an accident! Sometimes that smell of melting wax covered wires, along with the *'Bang'* of a bursting fuse, was orchestrated!

For example, it was very easy to wire up an exchange fuse to an unused telephone number. On dialling the number, the fuse would blow and raise an alarm. If the exchange was unmanned this alarm would be seen at a central point; and the engineer on night 'call out' would cash in on some nice overtime.

So, when you were on night 'call out' and there was nothing worth watching on television. All you had to do was dial your special number and wait a few minutes for your services to be requested! All this is theoretical of course, honest!

As you would have gathered by now, the guys were constantly on the look out for a prank. And, with electric shocks, the tool of choice for this was the 'Megger'. This instrument of torture was designed to generate a high voltage through a connected circuit for fault finding.

Basically the Megger was a brown wooden box, or sometimes a nice mottled Bakelite one, with a winding handle on one side. Winding of the handle generated a high voltage from the two wires coming from the side of the box. These wires each had connecting crocodile clips attached.

The real reason for this bit of kit was supposed to be measuring insulation resistance. However, it did have other uses. I only ever saw this devise being used for a fault once, and not appropriately. A suspected short circuit at the rear of a Strowger rack was located by connecting and winding the Megger like a 'man possessed'. The resultant melting wax wires could be smelt first; then a shower of sparks exposed the location of the fault.

It didn't take long for this devise to become both the prank of choice, and trial by combat. Picture the scene; you are one side of the MDF stripping back the wires of a jumper for connection. Your 'chums' are, unknown to you, connecting the other end of the jumper, unseen, to the Megger. Now you think this is a disconnected piece of wire. So you are not too careful how you handle it. Suddenly *'Whack!'*...your 'chums' had wound the handle and given you a nice wake-up call.

Yet again,

"Ouch! You fucking bastards!" would echo the Hill as yet another victim 'enjoyed' the joke.

I do not know what would have happened if anyone with a weak heart had suffered this experience. It could have killed them or maybe even cured them! After all, it was an early form of 'Electrical Cardioversion' or even a manual pacemaker!

This fun was not enough for the guys. They were bored and always looking for the next challenge. The Megger provided this challenge in the form of trial by combat. Who could hang on the longest?

Holding the wires with their hand, while a colleague wound the handle, usually lasted only a few seconds. But, with gritted teeth, and bulging eyes they hung on till the last nanosecond! Some challenges introduced some interesting suggestions for places to clip the Megger. Thankfully, they were dumb, but not that dumb!

So, bangs and pops were commonplace but, when unexpected, could be a bit unsettling. This was aptly demonstrated when I brought a small starting pistol to the Hill to 'test' reactions.

Again it was poor, long suffering Arthur who was the victim. There was a fault in-between two racks of his ageing, beloved Strowger equipment. The wiring behind these racks was fragile, to say the least, and normally left untouched. Only Arthur dared to poke around within. Because looking for one fault normally generated three others!

Now the gap between the racks was small, just enough for a ladder and body to squeeze into. Also behind these racks lay 33 years of dust. The fronts were cleaned, the rear never. So manoeuvring behind the racks was a tight, dirty job.

Arthur was half way up a ladder probing among

the ageing wires, aided by a head lamp. I was at the front armed with a small calibre starting pistol. The resulting *'BANG'* made his feet leave the ladder with a,

"AAAH! What the fuck was that?"

This, unfortunately, caused him to jerk his head backwards; thus dislodging the head lamp that was now firmly fixed over one of his eyes. This also, unfortunately, had the effect of dislodging a huge cloud of ancient dust. This dust now gently descended and settled all over Arthur.

He emerged from between the racks a bit shaken; 81s in one hand, a piece of wire in the other. His face impaired by a dislodged head lamp and his body covered in dust! Pocketing the pistol I exclaimed,

"Bloody hell Arthur, what caused that?"

"Honestly mate, I never touched anything," he explained.

"It just shows you how bloody dangerous this old stuff is," he added!

Whilst the lads found this funny, I decided that this particular prank could lead to disaster, so never brought the pistol back. Arthur never poked about in the rear of the racks again, and constantly warned others of the dangers!

CHAPTER 19-External Holes and Climbing Poles

My time had come for another 'experience' outside. This time the 'experience' was joining the cable gang for one week. This opportunity also included helping the telephone pole tester; Harry, for a day.

The cable gang team basically spent their lives pretending to pull out massive defunct or faulty cable runs and replacing them with new ones. When I say spent their lives, I mean between breakfast, tea, coffee and lunch breaks. This was heavy work and could be very laborious. Reconnecting hundreds of pairs of wires from an old cable to a new one could be mind numbing. Thank God I knew what the colour slate was!

This was often not a straight forward job as most of the manhole access points seemed to be continually flooded. Thus hours of pumping out were needed. Imagine the excitement for a young guy; sat watching water pump out of manhole for 3 hours. It was during this 'adventure' that I decided that only work in the exchange would keep me with the GPO.

There also appeared to be some considerable hazards with this role. Hazards that I had not known existed. It was quiet normal to find gas at the bottom of these manholes. I am talking here of gas of the variety that could kill you. Or gas of the variety that could blow you up. This stuff would seep naturally out of the ground and could accumulate dangerously in the ducts and manholes.

So, gas testing was generally undertaken before entry, or should have been! A couple of years later, in a location near the Hill, an engineer had sat with his feet down a manhole. The engineer in question unfortunately had a cigarette dangling from his mouth. The resultant blast just sent him flying backwards; and for several hundred yards down the road adjoining manhole covers flew into the air.

This 'event' resulted in some very near misses for some pedestrians and caused damage to cars. Miraculously nobody was injured, it could have been much worse.

Just to make me feel safe, and at home, the guys explained some further perils. A few months previously at the major traffic lights further up the road. A three man gang were re-running a cable.

The manhole this time was at the side of the road, so, their lorry had been strategically placed to guard the work.

Being coffee time, one of the guys was sent to fetch sandwiches from the local cafe. This cafe was about 20 metres from the site thus would only take a minute or so. Unfortunately, the engineer in question preferred sandwiches from the 'breakfast' cafe near the Hill. So off he drove with the lorry to fetch the supplies.

This manoeuvre was unknown to the others working down the hole. So, as the minutes passed, a head was poked out to investigate the delay. A passing car ran into the unsuspecting engineer and decapitated him.

I heard this same story many times and each time the details became more gruesome. However, the learning point was clear enough. This job could be really dangerous.

The rest of my week with these guys was spent with me looking for passing cars and continually sniffing for gas. However sat in their little tent casually blocking everyone's pathway on the pavement, I did learn something very useful. This was how to successfully cheat at the card game 'chase the lady'. This, more than anything else, came in very handy for future years in the Hill's canteen!

I also became bemused by their other favourite pastime. This was betting on the colour of knickers worn by passing ladies. Pavement manholes are most excellent for this game. A quick glance up at a passing victim was all that was required!

At least 50% of passing traffic could be verified by this method; however, the actual percentage of correct guesses was a lot lower. I think some of the colours mentioned were more wishful thinking than scientific 'form' reading. Naturally, they were all waiting for the obvious; no knickers. I am not sure however where this featured in the betting. Also I did wonder what would happen if a guy in a kilt had wandered past. I think it would have been eyes firmly on the cable and their talk changed to deep gruff voices for a few minutes!

My day out with Harry the telephone pole tester was enlightening. How on earth do you test a pole? What was the scientific approach? How complex was the technical equipment? Would I be baffled by the advanced technology of it all? After all, we had sent men to orbit the moon.

Well the scientific, technologically advanced equipment was a hammer! This guy basically bashed the bottom of the telephone pole with a hammer. If it sounded 'duff' it was marked for changing and a future pole changing team would, one day, arrive. If the pole sounded okay, well then it must be okay, mustn't it.

He tried to demonstrate this several times on both good poles and known bad ones. I could not tell the difference, and I was beginning to suspect that neither could he. So here we were judging the safety of lofty telephone poles (You know! the ones that engineers climb to the very top of!) with a hammer!

I had a similar 'technology' experience a few months later while out with the pressurised cable testing engineer. Some of the main telephone cables were pressurised from the exchange with air. This being the proven method for stopping water leaking into the cable and causing faults. If a cable air leak occurred, the air pressure fell and water could find its way in causing damage.

Helpfully warned by a pressure alarm in the exchange, off went our hero to locate the fault. Again I pondered on the highly advanced, technical solution to air leak detecting. I imagined a piece of kit resembling a sophisticated dash board. At the very least something with knobs and dials!

I was rather disappointed, therefore, to discover that it was an ancient, cracked coffee mug filled with very soapy water. This was applied to the cable with an equally ancient paint brush; a bubble immediately blowing once the air leak was found!

Back to hammers and poles, you can imagine my excitement when Harry mentioned that it was time for my telephone pole climbing experience! Now, prior to this particular week, news had leaked back from a recent TTA training course concerning poles. It also, unfortunately, concerned one of the guys I had started with.

The telephone poles at the training school were not lofty. They were not tall. At the top you were only about 3 metres off the ground. These poles were for learning the connection of overhead wire; drop wire as it was called. And for discovering the techniques of climbing, descending and use of the safety belt.

One rule was always taught, no finger rings! The guy in question had followed all the instructions, followed all the guidance and all the rules; bar one. On his little finger proudly sat a gold ring. On descending the pole, using the metal foot/hand pegs, he decided to jump the last half a metre or so. Unfortunately, as his feet left the pole, the ring caught on a metal peg further up.

The full weight of his body now pulled against a small, overlooked gold ring positioned carefully on his little finger. This ring, of course, currently being stuck to an immovable metal peg a few metres off the ground.

The result was both gruesome and catastrophic. The finger was torn away from his hand and, although rushed to hospital, was not saved.

So, coming back again to my excited face on hearing the news of my first ascent; you will gather by now that the excitement was not particularly of the good variety.

Harry had the perfect pole for this experience. It was a bit off the patch but perfect. Not far away was a road called Spring Hill. Now, the word hill was a give-away and I knew this place well. As a kid we used to free-wheel our bikes down this hill reaching about 100 miles per hour before the bottom. It was steep, very steep.

About half way down Spring Hill was a very tall telephone pole. It was tall but looked as though it was leaning dangerously to one side. This was the optical illusion caused by the steepness of the hill. An optical illusion that increased the further up you ascended.

Access to the first metal foot pegs was via a ladder, carefully placed against the pole by Harry. This ladder had to be propped up on one leg to compensate for the hill; thus looked extremely unsafe. Harry, however, did tie it off at the top...just for safety! He also helpfully tapped the bottom of the pole with his hammer. Just to demonstrate how safe it all really was! Did I imagine it or did this tapping sound a bit like one of the bad poles from earlier?

Now, at this point in my life I did not wear rings. I had never worn a ring. I had not even thought of wearing a ring. But I checked to make sure there were none on my fingers. I checked at the bottom of the ladder and I checked again at the top of the ladder. I was taking no chances.

At the top of the ladder the whole thing looked

precarious, however, after some gentle encouragement from Harry, I continued. Once on the pole itself I gripped the metal pegs like a man possessed and each step became more and more guarded.

At this stage the first evidence of gentle swaying was noticed, this along with an unnerving observation. The ground to my right looked a lot closer than the ground on my left! However, I checked for rings once more and climbed on.

After what seemed like two weeks I reached the top, the target had been achieved and I could relax. Well no actually. At the top this bloody thing was swaying, and the illusion of leaning heavily to one side was overpowering. Also my knees were beginning to shake. So, without instructions from Harry, I was on my way down; a lot faster than I went up. Getting onto the ladder was a good feeling; reaching the floor was a better one. But it still took a few moments to stop shaking.

"There you go," said Harry, "that's the worst you will ever climb!"

"Were you scared the first time you climbed it?" I enquired.

"Me! Fuck off! There's no way you would get me up there," declared Harry!

CHAPTER 20-Kiosk Scams and Drawing Pins

It was decided that I had need of some more external 'experience'. This time Stan had chosen Arthur the Kiosk engineer to be my mentor. Arthur or Art as everyone seemed to call him, was a gent, a character and pretty smart. His days with the GPO were coming to an end and retirement approached. Thus he continually was planning for the next adventure. For him this took the form of a bungalow on the Isle of Wight.

His little green van was stacked with coloured brochures of the island, along with detailed descriptions of available houses. This was to the detriment of available space for spare parts for his day job. He later admitted that all this was in the van because his wife had become pissed off. She had banned all this stuff from the house and I could see why.

Dressed in his usual dapper country jacket with handkerchief protruding from the top pocket; he would habitually raise his cap to just about everyone. And, as a consequence, everyone seemed to know him.

Everywhere we went it was,

"Hello Art, what's happening?"

He really seemed to be the local celebrity. Art, in fact, was a jack of all trades out on this patch. He would install, repair or fix phones but his real expertise was kiosks and PBX's (Private Branch Exchange). Now these were still the days of black A&B kiosk coin boxes. They were solid and reliable but vulnerable.

An easy, often used scam was to jam a strategically placed piece of card in the coin slot. Countless folk would try to push in coins but these would get jammed. And no amount of pushing the 'coin return' button returned anything.

These 'doctored' boxes were reported by their users as faulty. However before any engineer could arrive the 'mystery jammer' had returned. He had pulled out the offending card, pressed the coin return button and pocketed a large amount of cash.

The first day out with Art we found a jammed A&B box. This was before it had been reported and was by pure fluke. He was actually using the kiosk to call the exchange for updates!

Expertly removing the card he retrieved the cash and dialled the operator. Explaining the need for her to count money into the box, he slotted in half of the hoard, and kept the rest. Rushing round all the local kiosks we found a similar story. Our 'jammer' had been busy and we spent half a day pumping half of retrieved cash into the A&B boxes.

At this stage I was beginning to think that Art was going to keep his half of the hoard, and I was mentally counting my share. However, back at the exchange his reasoning became clear. Already a small disgruntled queue was forming demanding recompense for lost coins. Art's experience had taught him that 50% of folk phone in and complain; the remainder rush to the exchange to demand a refund. His little hoard just about paid these folk all back.

The GPO's own 'specialist' division were informed of this occurrence and, with the help of the police, this guy was quickly caught. For Art it was just another day in the office.

He seemed to have a few PBX client sites where Art would visit for some regular maintenance. Two in particular stick in the mind for varying reasons. The first was Holloway Prison, not far away in lington. It was an all female prison, famous as the place Ruth Ellis was hanged. She was the last woman to be hanged in the UK.

Before we arrived Art warned me of the long walk. I didn't understand the implication of his warning until we parked up inside and strolled across the yard. Cat calls, whistles, shouts and general sexual suggestions bombarded us from all angles. As a young inexperienced guy this was a bit unnerving to say the least. I just looked straight ahead, followed Art, shrinking smaller with each step. As we arrived at the main building he turned and said,

"You seem quite popular mate!"

"Thanks for that," I replied, as I glanced over my shoulder checking for the exit!

The walk out was certainly faster than the walk in and, thankfully, I never returned.

The second site that I have 'dined out' on many times was the local Tottenham nick. They had a small PBX downstairs, located in an unused cell! The small number of switches on the PBX had to be maintained and Art had lined me up for this boring job. Basically, contact cleaning.

Now the rules, as explained to me by the desk sergeant, were clear. All cell doors were to be locked at all times. I think I missed his wink at the departing Art. So, there I was locked in a prison cell having to yell every time I needed to get out. Naturally, every time I yelled, so did the various overnight drunks!

This went on for a couple of days and I was well pleased to get away. Clearly I had been tricked and I am sure Art and the sergeant had a good laugh at my expense. However, I could now claim to have genuinely been 'banged up' in jail!

It amazed me, at the time, how Art seemed to know every fault before we got anywhere. A disconnection was correctly identified to the actual manhole; line noise was correctly identified to another. He was not only doing this for our faults but for other engineers as well. Often, one would come up to us in the cafe, explain a problem, and go away with the solution.

One mind boggling solution highlights this ability. Sitting in the cafe, one of the other guys mentioned a strange fault that he was on his way to. Apparently every morning at about 10.00 am the subscriber's phone went dead. Everything in the exchange tested okay so the fault was out there somewhere.

Without even stopping to think about this, Art came out with,

"Dry joint, in the box, top of the building."

"What!" replied the baffled engineer, "how could you know that?"

"Wait and see," Art said.

After the recipient of this advice had left, Art leaned forward to explain. Apparently, overnight condensation can help a poor connection, but the morning sun dries this out and causes the fault! He had seen it before, it seemed so simple, but everyone else was left scratching heads!

This was not magic though; Art had been on this patch for a very long time. He knew every manhole, every flooded cable and every 'dry' joint. It made me wonder, what was going to happen when all the old lags like Art were gone?

His 'piece de resistance' came on the last day. We had started off as normal with Art receiving a nice piece of fish for changing a phone at the local fishmongers. There was nothing wrong with the phone, it was just completely covered and encrusted by months of smelly fish scales!

As this was a repeating problem, Art simply swapped out the phone every few months. This avoided customers phoning in and engineers being called out. He did admit though, that the real reason he did it was to see the faces of the store men when he returned the stinking old phone back to base! Personally, I think it was for the free fish!

On this particular day he picked up a new fault at his workshop, the kiosk. The phone in an office nearby had gone dead and they were in urgent need of help, business was being lost. On the way there he leant over to me and said,

"Drawing pin through the telephone wire!"

I smiled and decided that he had gone too far this time. On arriving at the office he tested the phone, it was okay, but the line was 'shorted out' i.e. the pair of wires were touching each other and causing the fault. He started to back trace the telephone wire along the wall; suddenly he stopped, pulled out a drawing pin from the cable and returned to the phone.

He tested the phone and found all to be working okay. With the usual thanks accepted we were quickly back off to the van; a smirk on his face, a puzzled look on mine. The whole thing had taken about 4 minutes.

"How the hell did you know that?" I enquired.

"Christmas mate, Christmas," he said, laughing at my puzzled look.

"I don't understand," I admitted, rather sheepishly. "Christmas was awhile ago."

"Christmas decorations, mate, either when they pin them up or when they finally pull the decorations down; happens every year!" he explained.

It would have taken me hours to find that fault and was another lesson. You just cannot beat experience.

Art retired from the GPO the next year, sold his nice little house in Seven Sisters Road and moved to the Isle of Wight. Reports came back from time to time that he was really enjoying himself and the length of time for fault finding in the area doubled!

CHAPTER 21-Oildag and Flooding Woes

One of the advantages of working at the exchange was the opportunity there to change everyday items into entertainment. The first victims of this were the green metal tool boxes. They were big, heavy, lockable and stacked with unused tools. They could be picked up by the metal handles at each end, and were constantly moved around.

The constant joke was to open these boxes up, drill holes through the bottom and screw them to the bench. Then, to add insult to injury, they would be locked shut with the lock hole soldered up! The owner would walk by, grabbing the handles as they passed, and end up pulled off their feet by the immovable box.

After swearing loudly at everyone within hearing distance; there would follow a battle with a hot soldering iron to free up the lock. This task was undertaken while questioning the parenthood of everyone else. As the box owner struggled with the hot iron and screwdriver an engineer with a ripped dustcoat would pass, and scold the box owner for falling for such an old trick!

Luckily for us all the GPO in its wisdom decided, with its new 1969 'branding', to change green tool boxes to yellow. Thus an excuse was there to get rid of the hole-ridden old boxes and book out nice new yellow ones!

Another item of fun was the humble 'Oildag'. This black sticky substance was the lubrication of choice for Strowger equipment.

Now, it may have been great for lubrication but it was even better for practical jokes. You have to bear in mind that nearly every phone in the building was black. You also have to remember that 'Oildag' was black. So an obvious stunt was a continual hazard, and drove the older guys crazy. I mean, obviously, painting everyday items with the stuff.

Picture the scene. The special faults phone rings, you answer the phone, there is no one there, and you replace the phone to return to the window. There you stand for the afternoon with a black ear. Someone else walks by with a black ear and you laugh; how could they fall for that!

It was not just phones though. It could be the underside of tool box handles, the inside of your mug handle, under door handles and so the list goes on. You had to be on constant guard and check everything. (Even now, if I pick up a black phone, I check it!) Stan was constantly impressed by the continual need to order this stuff. The guys must be working hard!

Due to this 'need', a two gallon can of Oildag was hidden down in the basement. (Stan was taking no chances) This oilcan became quite a star later into my apprenticeship. As I rode into the street leading to the exchange, I had to brake hard. Something was wrong, very wrong; it was a river. Being a conscientious type and knowing that the red line was about to be drawn, I parked up and waded to work.

A water main had burst almost immediately in front of the exchange, and water was still pouring out. Police were helping folk from houses and firemen were setting up pumps. This was not looking good; the coffee room was in the basement!

Luckily the telephone exchange designers had thought of this scenario and the doors into the cable chamber and boiler room were, when shut, water tight. This may have explained why we always nearly suffocated during film shows!

However, our coffee room was sunk.

Water Board engineers stopped the leak and began to dig around the offending area. As this was going on firemen were furiously pumping out the basement of the exchange. They had been convinced by the guys that the exchange would blow at any minute. The reality being, it was very nearly coffee time.

We, of course, used this as an excuse to fill every window with faces. It was not often that there was actually something worth watching out there.

Meanwhile Tiny was pacing frantically up and down. His boiler was down there, it could be drowning and it needed his help. What we didn't know, at the time, was that Tiny couldn't remember if he had closed the boiler room door or not! He was desperate to get down there before anyone else to check.

After an hour or so the water level was dropping, and you could make out the tops of the door frames down the basement stairs. All Tiny had to do was walk into the water up to his chest, (anyone else's waist) push his hand down into the water, and feel if the door was shut or not. His plan being to pull it shut if it was open and blame faulty door seals for a drowned boiler.

We were all up at the windows, the police were chatting up some girls from up the road and the firemen were all by their fire engine watching the Water Board guys dig. Here was Tiny's chance and in he went. After all, who would ever know?

He emerged triumphant, the door was actually already closed and his job was safe. But the secrecy of his mission was not. Across the front, back and sides of his chest and arms was a thick black sticky mess. It was also streaked up from his boots to his armpits.

As the water level slowly dropped further, his black sticky hand print could be clearly seen at the top of the boiler room door. And from the ceiling downwards the sticky residue could be seen.

Stan had left the lid of the Oildag can unscrewed and the contents had gradually risen to the top of the water. All the walls were streaked in the stuff. Tiny was streaked in the stuff and our coffee room was streaked in the stuff. When we realised what had happened Stan was given a round of applause for the best Oildag stunt ever pulled!

CHAPTER 22-Fire Proof Sacks and Physical Jerks

Here comes one of the brighter ideas from telephone exchange designers. Large cable runs between floors in the exchange needed large holes. These large holes presented, apparently, a fire hazard. So, their solution was to simply stuff these holes with a fire proof substance. The fire proof substance of choice was rough sacks filled with white asbestos!

Now don't get me wrong; we loved them. And the designers, I really hope, had no idea of the dangers at that time. Can you imagine the fun we had throwing these around. Football had a whole new meaning when clouds of dust erupted at each kick. As a punch-bag they couldn't be beaten. Each punch would cause an explosion. I remember one afternoon Arthur was returning from the lunch break. We had been throwing these around and I couldn't resist it,

"Hey! Arthur, catch," I said.

He very nearly did, but luckily he had seen all this

before. A quick sidestep avoided being enveloped in a dust shower.

"Fucking idiots!" was his nicely thought out, well tried and tested reaction.

Looking back now he was absolutely right. Through ignorance we were dicing with death. Every time I now read of the dangers and perils of working with asbestos, I think back to those guys. How many of them eventually paid the ultimate price for this sky lark?

Some months later, unannounced, a white van pulled up outside the exchange. Two guys with white overalls appeared. They donned rubber boots, rubber gloves and, were we seeing things, breathing apparatus. They entered the exchange, passed a written explanation to Bernie and prepared their plastic bags. There followed half a day of asbestos removal, one by one the asbestos sacks disappeared.

We all watched this silently, puzzled by the suddenness of it all. It wasn't till some time later that the truth came out. This had happened to all the old exchanges. The cat was out the bag as to the dangers of asbestos, and the GPO had quickly and quietly removed the offending evidence!

There were many other diversions available to the bored youth that inhabited Stamford Hill exchange. One of the more competitive was physical fitness. Amongst the racks of equipment you would often find pull-up bars, punch bags and a variety of other home made gym equipment. Hours were spent with push ups and pull ups with much banter as to who was best.

The older engineers, of course, found this highly amusing but somewhat irritating. Looking back I can see how their world of work and responsibility was gradually being eroded. This caused by the new kids on the block who just wanted to have a laugh. They really did not know how to handle it, should they join in or tow the corporate line.

I guess you did not need a great deal of intelligence to work out the obvious. That if no work was being done yet everything continued to function okay; why did you need 30 engineers there? The truth of course was clear; you didn't!

One particular morning we were in fierce combat with pull-ups. Ben was always best. With biceps bulging, eyes popping and a strained concentration on his face, he could deliver 50 plus excellent pull-ups. Something that was hard to match even with arms honed on lifting paraffin cans. As we took it in turns to try our cleaner, old Bill, came ambling along pushing his broom across already clean floors.

He was in his 60's, an ex soldier who always tut-tutted at our antics and bollocked us continually if we dared drop anything on his floor. Of course, to us, he looked about 100 but this morning he was about to make us all feel deficient.

As he approached the group he casually leant his broom on the side of the equipment rack, stepped up to the bar and jumped up. There followed 30 clean pull-ups without a grunt or puff. He dropped back to the floor. Picked up his broom, and continued on his way along the floor, cleaning as he went.

He had not spoken a word and nor had we. In fact there followed a deathly silence as a tableau of frozen faces watched him disappear through the racks of equipment.

"Fucking hell!" was all that was said as we broke up to rush off to the next coffee break.

It took the gloss off future competitions and our older colleagues never let us forget it.

Old Bill's other constant nag was the ever growing pile of discarded old phones in the yard. He was forever trying to tidy it up only to find loads more dumped the following day. These were mostly black Bakelite phones from the 30s, 40s and 50s. Some were broken, some had parts missing but others were complete. As the engineers changed these phones for new plastic ones, the original plan was return them to stores. But the stores did not want them. Nobody wanted them, so there they were, a pile growing higher by the day.

Now, in amongst that pile were old candlestick phones and Bakelites of several colours. Today they would be worth hundreds of pounds each. It is with some sadness, then, that I recall the day that a lorry arrived. The phones were removed and dumped somewhere in a landfill. This happened across the many hundreds of exchanges hoarding this stuff!

Somewhere, someone is probably living in a house on a 70's built housing estate; calmly sipping tea over countless thousands of valuable old telephones!

CHAPTER 23-Sick Leave and All's Quiet

One of the more interesting discoveries when joining a Civil Service establishment was enlightenment on organisation. I am not talking about managerial organisation here; rather how the guys organised the below the radar stuff. Take sick leave for example. You get sick, you stay off work, and you come back well again. Oh! No; it didn't work that way. When you were sick you came in to work. What's the point of being at home when you were ill?

Time off for sick was a 'Whitley'. Carefully guarded, controlled and organised to perfection by the unofficial management.

John Henry Whitley was tasked by the government in 1917 to form joint industrial councils to discuss and agree all aspects of working life. These 'Whitley Councils', as they became known, sort of failed in most industries. However, in the vast armies of Civil Service life, they flourished. And, the GPO was Civil Service!

Whatever the original correct agreement about

time off for sickness, two weeks a year was deemed acceptable under the auspices of Whitley agreements. At least, that duration was everyone's understanding. Thus, alongside your yearly annual leave entitlement there was the additional two weeks off sick!

Now the management team may have had control over annual leave and the cover thereof. But, it was the guys who ensured sick leave was scheduled, controlled and most importantly taken. This perfect arrangement all came back to haunt me many years later when, as Head of HR, I had to remove it from their mindset.

Typically John, one of the senior TOs, would ask if it was leave or Whitley; this in response to my mentioning a few days off. If I answered leave he would immediately ask how much Whitley I had left. It was made quite clear that not taking your allotted Whitley days was somehow letting the team down! I am certain that Mr John Henry Whitley would have spun in his grave to learn that 'official' skiving off was forevermore legitimised in his name!

The other well organised underground scheduled activity was overtime. This opportunity was vital for most of the guys as they all would budget their lives around receiving it. Thus without it, they were screwed. Now this shouldn't have been a problem except for one blatantly obvious reality. If we got by during the week doing not a lot, where was the work for overtime? The answer was clear. Doing the things that we should have been doing through the week!

Now here it gets a bit complicated so, pay attention. Why on earth would we want to spend Saturday or even Sunday actually working? We could be playing snooker. So it was clear to all that the overtime work needed to be completed before Saturday arrived. To that end, after a work schedule for the weekend had been agreed, we would rush about and do this work by close of play Friday.

So, when watching the guys pulling jumpers, changing relays and cleaning Strowger on a Friday. What you were actually seeing was them doing the work they should have been doing. That is before it had been re-scheduled for Saturday. Thus they were actually working normally and leaving Saturday a free day. Get it?

Now, naturally, this being the GPO the guys quickly took this to the next level. Things to do on overtime were prepared and left for Stan to organise. What happened after that was for us to organise. And it didn't take long for an attendance rota to be drawn up.

I mean, if there was nothing left to do on Saturday, why waste time playing snooker. You could be at home watching the wife working. So only one or two guys actually turned up. They signed the signing-on book for everyone and headed for the top of the MDF for a snooze.

The phone would be answered, reluctantly, and a few games of snooker would be played. Then after lunch they disappeared. The rota ensured we all took turns with this laborious task and the chances of anyone finding out were slim. Bernie, for example, wasn't seen during the week let alone the weekend. And Stan sort of accepted it. So, with a few phone numbers for emergencies this practice went on for quite a while, right up to the moment Bernie retired!

Poor Bernie, he always dreamed of extending his time with the GPO beyond retirement age. This had nothing to do with his love of telecommunications, of course, he needed his office! However, his private business, the wage snatch, the flood and the erratic nature of the Hill's performance caused questions to be raised. The chaos caused by bus queue soakings didn't help either.

The final straw came following the big crash! Now, this wasn't his fault actually; it was just on his watch. The timing of this event was bad, a few weeks before Christmas, and the Hill was quiet. Everyone had left bar a few of us stretching out some evening overtime. I had finished mine and was idly playing solitaire with my marked deck. Sid and John were close to finishing; and in a while we all would have gone home. Yes, the Hill was quiet, in fact too quiet!

It occurred to all three of us at the same moment. Why was the Hill quiet, it was never quiet, it was a Strowger exchange! Something was wrong, very wrong. Nothing was working, no alarms, no calls, nothing. Rushing about like headless chickens didn't seem to help much. And no amount of picking up phones seemed to alter the fact, the Hill was dead!

Now, here's a thing. How can you call for assistance when the very thing that generates the calls is dead? So, we were stuck and had to soldier on. Getting back to basics we checked the power supply. There wasn't any, and a rush down to the power room explained why. Two huge fuses supplying power to the equipment had blown; next to their smouldering remains hung two new standby ones. So, with great speed we changed these and stood back. *'BANG'* they went the way of their friends and blew!

We all looked at each other and chanted *'Shit',* in unison. You have to remember that this was in the days before cell phones, we were screwed. Now, a team of power engineers had been working on the batteries and power racks that day, so, it was not rocket science to guess the cause. Remember the lesson from chapter four? *'Don't Touch Anything!'*

John jumped in his car and left for Tottenham exchange, not far away. We sat looking at each other in the eerie silence that is dead Strowger. Many phone calls from Tottenham raised an emergency power team, probably the same guys that were at the Hill during the day. But they would be a couple of hours. So, Stamford Hill Automatic Telephone Exchange was off air for the first time in 33 years. And we had been told to stay until relieved!

It was really creepy wandering around a dimly lit exchange with absolutely no noise. I did not help matters when I decided to stand behind the test desk switchboard, with my head resting on the top.

So from the front, it looked like someone had placed a severed head on top of the switchboard.

In the gloom Sid ambled round the corner, saw my head, and screamed,

"AAAH! Fuck! You stupid bastard!"

I don't know why, but he didn't seem to think it was funny!

It was with great relief that we watched the power guys arrive and restore the electric supply; and the Hill slowly, very slowly came back to life. With that life we experienced the noise and hundreds of alarms from a complaining Strowger. It took us another two hours to get the exchange back to normal, and we were knackered.

It was on my way home that I suddenly thought,

'So, the power guys come in, mess with the power equipment, leave and are then called out in the night on expensive overtime!'

Now I am not pointing an accusing finger at subterfuge here, just saying!

The next day the Hill was descended upon by the big brass. It really was unheard of for an exchange to be off air, and Bernie was under the cosh. It didn't help his cause when asked to ensure a big team was left during the night, just in case. He politely explained that it was our Christmas do and they would have to find engineers from somewhere else!! The big brass left blue in the face and Bernie was doomed.

At least we stopped him from being killed that night. On entering the club hired for our do; he pushed our entry tickets into the hands of the doormen. Unfortunately, they were not doormen. They were two uniformed merchant seamen. And these two guys took great exception to being mistaken, in their uniforms, for doormen!

Blood was prevented from being spilled by our numbers, and John buying them several drinks. I don't think that Bernie even noticed. Early the next year, when I returned to work from a motorbike accident, he was gone!

The aftermath of this motorbike accident is worth a mention. I was off work for a month or so with a bad gash to the head. This followed a collision with a car at some traffic lights along Green Lanes. My crash helmet had undoubtedly saved my life.

An EE was dispatched to check me out. Basically was I still technician material or was I now destined for the stores. How caring!

After he had ensured that I was still 'Compos Mentis' he got up to leave but stopped at the door. There he turned and casually informed me that one of the guys I had joined with had not been so lucky. He also had a motorbike accident but was dead. Well, thanks for breaking it so gently my friend.

CHAPTER 24-Kite Chaos and Winning Horses

My dad had always been a bit of a boffin, always inventing things. His current project was making devices that could propel a camera up a flying kite string to take overhead pictures of Clissold Park. Don't ask me why, I have no idea.

This kite flying was a bit of a passion, and he could often be found in the park with a like minded group. Their kites would soar so high that you couldn't see them. So all you could see were several men quietly sat on string boxes glancing up to the sky, at nothing!

He made all his own kites and they really worked well. Some of them stood more than 6 feet tall, and all were intricate in design. Noticing one day how windy it was on the roof at the Hill; I had a thought. Perhaps instead of sunbathing I would fly a kite.

Now the problem with the guys at the Hill was that everything became a competition. So, as soon as I mentioned my idea, others declared an interest. And minutes after declaring this interest, arguments began as to who could fly the highest.

Now some of these guys had never flown a kite before. Some had never even seen a kite but it did not matter. By tea break that afternoon 10 had joined the group, and word was still spreading. By the time of the chosen day nearly 20 kites were making their way up to the roof and another 12 or so spectators were already passing 'expert' judgement on their manufacture.

The guy in our local hardware shop had run out of string, dale rods and cloth and was well pleased. The wind was up; we were ready, what could possibly go wrong?

As the 'brains' behind this venture my kite went up first. I had seen my dad do this countless times and at the first attempt it was up and rising. The string was housed in a large box which played out at an alarming rate. Luckily it had a brake and a geared winding handle, to one side, to wind this lot back in again. Others followed with varying success but generally they were all slowly ascending.

Now the fun started. When one kite is flying you do not experience many problems. When several kites are flying you may get a few tangles. When nearly 20 kites are in the sky; over a small roof, mostly flown by amateurs, you get chaos. Kites were crashing into the road, bouncing of bus roofs, disappearing into peoples gardens and generally going anywhere except where they should be going.

Some strings were snapping and their adjoined kites disappearing over the horizon. Others were burning flesh as they tore rapidly through unprotected hands. None were behaving themselves and this was quickly turning into bedlam.

As my kite had now disappeared behind a cloud, I was declared the winner and everyone was disappearing as fast as possible. Hands had to be salved, missing kites found and hundreds of knots undone. The scene on the roof now was of ripped cloth, broken dale rods, piles of broken knotted string and general mayhem. I finally retrieved my kite, in a now battered state, and crept away. It wasn't my kite, naturally, it was my dads and I had some explaining to do!

One of the other lunchtime pastimes was the horses. Most of the guys had a flutter from time to time. And big events always generated a sweepstake. This was the end of March, and that could only mean one thing, the famous Grand National. Yet no one had started a sweepstake; so I did. Now for some reason I had a slight reputation then as being a bit of a wide-boy. Rather unfounded I might add, I blame George and the Paraffin round.

So selling the tickets was somewhat difficult, everyone was looking for a catch. There was no catch, of course, you paid your money, pulled a ticket out of a box and that was that. With 45 runners I had enough tickets for all the engineers, some telephonists and a few external guys. I wanted a ticket myself so waited patiently for the last remaining one; that would be mine.

The race was held on a Saturday which fell nicely into place with our overtime leisure. A television was brought in, beers chilled, seating set up in the canteen and we were ready. Prizes were to be given for first, second and third places and tension was running high.

As usual, with this race, there were plenty of fallers and refusals. So, much shouting and banter was echoing round the room. Throughout the final few furlongs this reached a crescendo as the first three horses neared the line.

What nobody had noticed was me, glancing back and forth from the television screen to my ticket, and as the horses crossed the line you heard a general shout,

"So then, who has won?"

"Well Jimmy the fitter came third, and Linda the telephonist came second," I responded.

"Yes! But who won?" they impatiently replied.

"Er! I did!" I said.

"WHAT?" they all shouted at once.

"Look at my ticket, Red Alligator, it's mine," I explained with some hesitance.

"How the fuck did you pull that one?" they unhelpfully added.

And so it went on for about an hour. Close examination of my running order chart clearly showed my name against Red Alligator. Careful perusal of my ticket, even holding it up to the light, revealed nothing. I had won. And begrudgingly they all dispersed. No one said congratulations; ungrateful bastards!

A detailed, professional diagnosis of the race, my ticket, my parental background, the chart and known racing scams came to an inevitable conclusion. It was all above board, there was no way it could be a scam. However, they never let me run a sweepstake again!

Many years later I bumped into one of the guys at an event in London. He walked up and clasping my hand immediately said,

"Go on, you can tell me now; how did you do it?"

CHAPTER 25 – Spotty Mystery & First Aid Scam

While we were busily ignoring the old Strowger equipment the powers at the head of the mighty GPO were working hard on the next generation of equipment to take its place.

Electronics rather than mechanical switches were the future and not just for efficiency reasons. The next generation of exchange equipment would not need much maintenance and thus not many maintenance engineers. We, of course, were oblivious to this and the construction on the second floor of a large new equipment room generated little interest.

After all, what interest could a large empty nicely plastered parquet floored room hold for us. I mean, it just looked like a squash court! Oh dear, in fact it did look like a squash court and it did not take long for that similarity to have the inevitable effect.

Just a day after the painters had moved out, we moved in. There was, as yet, no electric lighting but the ample windows gave enough light to start the next lunchtime pastime and this time everyone joined in.

Now the guys had mostly never played squash before but it was an up and coming popular sport. Plus who needs proper squash racquets? Old tennis racquets, ageing badminton racquets or just a piece of wood would do. And a squash ball was cheap.

We hammered that room for weeks. The guys progressed from playing in hobnail boots to trainers, and from broken badminton racquets to real squash ones. The local sports shop must have thought that a revolution in squash was taking place as one after another telephone engineer arrived and demanded the cheapest squash racquet available. They had to ask of course because most of them didn't know what a real squash racquet looked like!

Table tennis and snooker were put on the back burner as more and more of the Hill's finest took up the new challenge. And not just the young guys; some of the old lags were up for it as well. However, their red faces pouring with sweat rather told its own story; this was going to kill someone.

Luckily fate overtook the impending health danger when it was announced that an official opening of the new 'Electronic Exchange Wing' was forthcoming. To this end electricians were prompted to begin their wiring up of the mass of fluorescent lights that littered the ceiling.

This of course put a stop to our sporting activities and we gracefully, somewhat begrudgingly returned to less frantic lunchtime pursuits. Car boot sales all over Hackney suddenly were awash with squash racquets. However one or two of us kept up the sport and I did go on to be somewhat accomplished at club level and even ironically represented BT in squash competitions; if only they had known!

Bernie took an interest in the great switch on of the lighting as a last ditch attempt at looking like he was interested in Stamford Hill. He even invited several other managers to witness the event; the grand lighting up of the latest in equipment rooms.

Many of us had gathered as the electricians completed the final wiring and ensured all was fused and ready. Then with a rather theatrical wave from Bernie the lights were switched on.

A rather long deathly hush fell on the assembled guests as they took in the sight. Vast white painted plastered walls with about two million green spots covering everything. Walls, ceiling, floors and even windows!

As none of us had ever entered a real squash court before, we had not realised that squash balls leave a mark. A green mark that is very difficult to remove. And our weeks of frantically hitting squash balls all over the new room had left it completely covered.

The marks were unnoticeable in the light provided by the windows but in the harsh reality of fluorescent lighting they stood out like a scratch on a new car. Bernie's big moment was yet another disaster. Quick as ever he recovered and explained that he knew about this and the painters had been bollocked and would be back to finish off the job properly. However the gloss on his day was gone.

Nobody actually got reprimanded for the mysterious green spots; after all how do you reprimand just about everyone in the exchange. Come to think of it, most of the engineers from nearby exchanges as well. However, the Hill never saw a squash ball again.

It was shortly after this further highlight in Bernie's career that Stan cornered me in the canteen. I thought for a moment that the chickens had come home to roost and my part in the squash chaos was about to be repaid. However, Stan had much more urgent business to discuss.

Stan, you see, was a first aid trainer. This was something he seemed to take very seriously, so much so that he often disappeared for weeks at a time under the banner of 'training'.

We knew nothing about this pastime or the implications of being involved but all was to become clear. Stan started by offering me one of his roll-ups, you know, the ones that he rolls up and leaves in various pockets for weeks on end. I had once seen someone light up a Stan roll-up. It was so dry and aged that the flame shot from one end to the other before the recipient could pull it out of his lips! Thus I passed.

He then mentioned the amount of overtime that he was securing for me and how he personally felt I was going to go far in the GPO. Oh! And by the way, did I want another cup of tea? Now, I may have been young but I wasn't born yesterday; Stan wanted something, there was a price to be paid.

Stan, in fact, was not just a first aid trainer he was the guy who historically had trained the first aid team for North Area London. This was the team that had always reached 3rd or 4th in the London First Aid Competition. Sometimes they had gone on with other London teams to fight for the National title. However, his team had broken up and a new one needed to be formed, and formed pretty damn fast. The next London competition was not far off.

He explained that as I had passed my life saving awards I must have covered some first aid. I cautiously admitted this to be the case. Mouth to mouth, cardiac arrest and recovery position had all been taught. Therefore, he continued, I would be perfect for the first aid team. I quietly thought this over with classic GPO mentality.

"What's in this for me then?" I casually enquired.

"Each Wednesday afternoon off training and one week off training before the competition" he countered.

I didn't need much more explanation than that; a week off messing about with bandages sold it. Thus I joined the other 'volunteers' to make up the 4 required for the new team. And what a team it was, never has such a group of ham fisted, know nothing idiots ever been brought together to enter a competition in the history of ...well...competitions actually!

The training quickly started and each week that

went by we progressed from hopeless to worse than hopeless and Stan shouted,

"Breathing, Bleeding, Broken Bones!"

so many times that I can still hear him now.

You see it was a bit more complex than a few bandages. It wasn't the scam I thought it would be. Complete scenarios were set up with crashed cars, blood, gore and screaming victims. We appeared to have an army of people to bandage up, all of whom had been tempted by the week off offer. Much fun was had but this was serious stuff and slowly we were coming to the inevitable conclusion; we were crap. All the information was there but we were just too lazy to take it in and this was just a laugh, wasn't it?

Stan was coming to the same conclusion and his reputation as a trainer looked like it was going to take a massive knock back. This was visible by the amount of roll-ups he was manufacturing and storing in the various pockets of his ageing jacket. They were bulging and once, in a fit of frustration, he almost lit one up!

It was at this low ebb that he had his epiphany

moment and his deep understanding of the psyche of his fellow engineers proved advantageous.

"Don't worry guys, it's all a waste of time anyway" he said.

"Why is that?" we responded in unison.

"Well, City area always win and there's nothing you could do to change that anyway" he continued.

"Why is that?" we responded in unison; again.

"Well they are heavily trained and just love walking off with the big trophy; and they are sort of used to the pictures in the press and stuff" he added, warming to the theme.

"What big trophy?" we enquired, suddenly becoming more interested.

"Well there's a big trophy for the winners and it's had City area's name on it for nearly 10 years. Anyway, they love the individual trophies you get to keep and performing in front of a big audience" he explained.

"Trophies you keep?" my three team mates exclaimed.

"Big audience?" I said at the same time.

"Yes, of course, lots of pictures holding up your trophies in the press and a big piece in the GPO journal" he continued.

"Lots of pictures?" asked my three team mates.

"What big audience?" I simultaneously asked now becoming rather nervous.

However, the seed had been sown. This was now personal and the whole training process was seen in a new light. It was a real competition and we were going up against an unbeatable team. Plus we were going up against them in front of a vast audience with the results being plastered in the local press and across the whole GPO population!

That week we actually started reading the first aid manuals. We started to listen to the tactics and advice. We began to really practice the myriad of different bandaging techniques. Jokes were put aside, lunch breaks were short and we even sat quietly watching films of past events. It was the first time any of us had watched a film on GPO premises that wasn't XXX rated.

Stan's plan had worked and whilst not really ready we would probable not make fools of ourselves. And more importantly for Stan, his reputation would survive; just.

The big event arrived along with teams from all parts of the complex system that formed the greater London GPO. It was when I saw the large number of teams involved along with the huge number of audience folk, and finally the army of patients, judges and helpers of every description; that I realised just how big the GPO organisation was.

Lots were drawn to decide what sequence the teams would go in, and just to get us off on a great start we drew last! This would mean we would have to sit in a locked up room, watching one team after another depart, for about 4 hours. But, unlike most of the others in the room, the guys continued their studies, asked ourselves probing questions and continued to focus on the job in hand. The dye was set and these guys were now serious.

We had taken Stan's advice and split ourselves

into two groups of two. This was because often the scene would involve several casualties of varying degrees of injury. Plus we had nominated our oldest team mate as 'number one' on the grounds that he lost our rock-paper-scissors competition the day before. You see, none of us wanted to go solo which was the fate of each team's 'number one' after the team had performed. Thus we cheated and pre-arranged the rock-paper-scissors hand selections accordingly! Sorry Jim if you're reading this!

Our time had come and we were ushered onto the stage. I was so frightened that I was oblivious to the hundreds of faces peering at us. I did notice one though; Stan, right down the front looking a bit pale.

The scene we were met with was a bit of a shock. The remnants of a smashed car obviously 'borrowed' from the local scrap metal dealer, and a crushed motorcycle all intertwined with bodies. Now, we had used fake blood in practice but these 'volunteers' had been professionally made up and they really did look the part. However, I managed to overcome the urge to throw up and we split up and set to work.

Our progress was being impeded by a casualty

who was pushing us, moaning rather loudly, screaming that he was in pain and generally getting in the way. All I could think of was to push him roughly on his backside, throw a blanket over his shoulders, stick a thermometer in his mouth, and tell him to be quiet. After all, the other guy on the floor was bleeding all over the place and Stan's 'Breathing, Bleeding, Broken Bones' was ringing in my ears.

I would come back to him in a minute. As I glanced up I could see Stan getting paler and his eyes were bulging. It must have been very hard for him not to shout out instructions but all he could do was watch.

Unfortunately, our 15 minute time allowance shot past in what seemed like seconds. As time was called we all slowly got up from our casualties to survey the scene. Well, we had got people breathing, we had stopped all the bleeding and those broken bones all looked pretty neat to me. It was then that I noticed him. He was still sat where I had pushed him down; still sat with a thermometer in his mouth. He had been left unattended to even though he was obviously in a lot of pain. I glanced over to Stan, who was now very red, shaking a bit with what I assumed was rage and rolling several roll-ups at once.

We were ushered to one side with polite applause as Jim had to continue with his solo challenge. If I wasn't so mortified at leaving one of the casualties alone for 15 minutes the 'number one' slot would have been laughable. It was a diabetic in a coma and Jim's brother was a diabetic. It was something he had been dealing with for years. He knew the signs, symptoms and recovery process better than most doctors. He smashed it without even having to think.

That was it. It was all over and Stan wandered up looking somewhat relieved.

"That idiot shouting that he was in pain" he opened with.

"Yes, look er! I'm sorry about that" I said, "only I just ran out of time"

"Everyone else spent ages on him" he continued, rather excitedly I thought.

"Yes, but I was going to come back to him, I just got a bit tied up with the others" I lied.

"Don't you understand you twat?" he continued. "There was nothing wrong with him, he was a diversion! Everyone else wasted ages on him!"

It suddenly dawned on me that somehow I was coming out of this without a bollocking; in fact, we were actually looking in good shape. As scores were calculated we all gathered to hear the announced results. Amongst the shouts I missed our actual score and turned to Stan for an update. He was stood rigid, an unlit roll-up dangling from his open mouth. "Fuck me!" was all I could get out of him and I was beginning to think he was going to pass out.

We had won! The trophy was ours, the pictures in the press were ours and that big piece in the GPO journal was all about us. We had our moment of glory, Stan had his moment of massive gloating with the trainer of City area and I had got away with murder.

As a parting gesture the head judge came up to me and congratulated me on my stunning tactic of quietening a hysterical casualty.

"Er, I'm not quite with you" I responded.

"Well, telling him to sit his arse down and shut the fuck up" he said "That brought him round;

classic!!"

During the following years life went on much as before. People came and went, pranks were played and general mayhem ruled. I gradually worked my way up through the grades until I earned that bowler!

However, I could not see my life, like the others, played out forever at Stamford Hill. My horizon was beyond the Hill and I left to pursue opportunities elsewhere.

In my entire long career I was never to meet such a bunch of characters again. In fact the bizarre experiences, idiotic decisions, and 'laissez-faire' attitudes were not encountered again until I moved to live in a small village in France. But that's another story!

EPILOGUE

I remember, as a teenager, hearing about the new Post Office Tower. It was futuristic, had a revolving restaurant and was posh. It was opened in 1965 by Harold Wilson and was the epitome of British cool. Throughout my early career I had no chance of getting anywhere near it and an IRA bomb shut it forever to the public in 1981.

Although it was called The Post Office Tower it was, in fact, commissioned by the GPO; thus had to continue with GPO idiocy. To this end it was designated an official secret and its existence not finally admitted to until 1993. This, despite standing 177 metres high in the middle of central London!

Yet here I was spinning round, enjoying a beautiful meal taking in the fabulous views. As a perk of being in a senior position I was able to book this place for various prestigious events and meetings; a perk I used whenever possible.

On this occasion it was a 'thank you' meal for the senior team in BT's networks. It had been a good year and we were celebrating success. I was stood fielding questions as to how a telephone apprentice ended up as Head of HR. The other management folk couldn't comprehend it. Well, actually neither could I!

One of the General Managers asked where I had started, to which I responded Stamford Hill. He seemed to know of the place, North Area London was on his patch and glumly he dropped the bad news that it was now just a shell. I mentioned that it was a shame as I would have liked to have seen the Hill again. He thought that this would not be a problem and, with that, we both moved on to the Champagne; not a pink cake in sight.

Back in the office the following Monday, I was somewhat surprised to find yet another meeting squeezed into a creaking diary. Now, good secretaries are a bit like doctor's receptionists, hard to get past. Hence an 'emergency' reason must have been sold to mine for the diary to change.

So the next day there I was stepping up to those big double doors once more. Nearly 20 years to the day since I had left. There to greet me was a rather nervous Level 2 or EE in old speak. (BT removed grades by simply calling them levels, how GPO!) His name was John and he was my guide. I didn't have the heart to tell him that I knew this place better than he ever would.

As we passed through the inner doors he said,

"Apparently there used to be a great sign on this door; Please Wipe Your Boots!"

"Shame," I replied, "someone must have nicked it!"

The Strowger had long since disappeared and the new digital equipment could have been housed in your shed. So, the Hill was quiet and empty. New equipment didn't need 30 engineers; well actually neither did the old stuff!

However, strangely, the smell was still there. It hit me immediately and the memories came flooding back. The ghosts of the lads laughing, joking and generally messing about could almost be heard; and my tinnitus kindly added the authentic background of Strowger. I could feel it; John couldn't.

He explained that the only thing left from the past was the MDF, and the test room. Jumpers, occasionally, still had to be changed. All else was gone, and this became apparent as we wandered around. The 'guide' role was reversed as I explained what most of the rooms were actually used for.

As we walked through the remnants of the test room I found a box of decaying old fault dockets. I couldn't resist looking through to see if one of mine were there. No luck though; thinking about it mine were all FNF, and all probably dumped!

At that moment I noticed two engineers pulling a jumper on the MDF, and I wandered up to have a look and say hello. Now here came a moment when true life can genuinely outplay fiction. On my last day at the Hill I wandered the floors saying goodbye to the guys. Our long haired hippie, Graham, was among the last and, as I left, he was up a ladder on the MDF waving.

Yet here he was, still up a ladder, still pulling jumpers! He could immediately be recognised by the white remains of his 'goatee', but all the hair had gone. Paired with a young technician he was valiantly trying to look busy as we approached. My greeting of,

"Hello Graham."

Stopped him dead and he responded with a surprised,

"Bloody hell mate, where have you been?"

I explained to John that I had known Graham from the old days and he politely wandered off so that we could have a chat. We swapped some old stories and laughed together at some of the antics; but sadly he brought me up to date with those who were no longer with us. So, it had been the ghosts of Bernie, Arthur, Stan, John, Art and others that I could feel on entering the Hill.

As a parting comment he mentioned his unsuccessful attempts to be given a lucrative 'early release' redundancy opportunity. Time was running out for this, and he feared he would miss the boat. Er! Coincidentally, he was offered this opportunity a few weeks later!

With the visit and our chat over, for the second time, I waved goodbye to Graham as he pulled his jumper through on the MDF. Passing through the door I could not resist it; I leant back and shouted,

"SLACK BACK!"

An audible snip was quickly followed by,

"Fuck it, FUCKING BASTARD!"

With that I descended the stairs and left the Hill for ever.

A final word:

Thank you for reading 'Please Wipe Your Boots' I hope you enjoyed the book as much as I enjoyed writing it.

If you could spare the time to leave a review with Amazon I would very much appreciate it. Reviews are the lifeblood for authors and help considerably with future projects.

At the moment I am busy writing the misadventures of a Londoner struggling with life in a small rural French village. The characters, unbelievable chaos, crazy antics and general mayhem mirror very closely my time with the GPO. Something I never believed could possibly be encountered again.

This new book will be ready for publication in the spring of 2016 and I am looking forward to its impact. A 'no holds barred' insight into the mentality of our French neighbours and what it is really like to live amongst them. There have been many books written about living in France; however, this is the one that may start WW3!

Stanley George

Printed in Great Britain
by Amazon